CHURCH FURNISHINGS
A NADFAS guide

D0132600

PATRICIA DIRSZTAY

illustrated by

CAROLINE COOK
FRANCES CURWEN
and
PAUL VINCENT

ROUTLEDGE & KEGAN PAUL
London and Henley

First published in 1978
by Routledge & Kegan Paul Ltd
39 Store Street,
London WC1E 7DD and
Broadway House,
Newtown Road,
Henley-on-Thames,
Oxon RG9 1EN
Printed in Great Britain by
Redwood Burn Limited
Trowbridge and Esher

British Library Cataloguing in Publication Data

Dirsztay, Patricia
Church furnishings.
1. Church decoration and ornament   2. Church
furniture
I. Title
247   NK1652

ISBN 0 7100 8820 5 (c)

ISBN 0 7100 8897 3 (p)

CONTENTS

PREFACE   vii

HOW TO USE THE GUIDE   ix

                                illustrated by

ARCHITECTURAL TERMS   Paul Vincent   1

BOOKS AND BOOKBINDING   Caroline Cook   10

BRASSES, ARMS AND ARMOUR   Caroline Cook   17

CERAMICS   Caroline Cook   25

CLOCKS   Frances Curwen   29

COSTUME   Caroline Cook   31

CREATURES AND ANIMALS   Caroline Cook   43

CROSSES AND CRUCIFIX   Caroline Cook   45

DECORATIVE MOTIFS   Caroline Cook   50

FLOWERS, FRUIT AND TREES   Caroline Cook   55

FRAMES   Frances Curwen   58

HERALDRY   Paul Vincent   59

LETTERING   Caroline Cook   72

MEMORIALS AND MONUMENTS   Paul Vincent   75

METALWORK   Frances Curwen   86

	illustrated by	
MISCELLANY	Frances Curwen	127
MUSICAL INSTRUMENTS	Caroline Cook	131
SAINTS, SCENES, SIGNS AND SYMBOLS	Caroline Cook	136
SANCTUARY	Paul Vincent	153
SHAPES	Frances Curwen	154
STONEWORK	Paul Vincent	161
TEXTILES	Caroline Cook	166
VESTMENTS including NAPERY	Caroline Cook	181
WALL PAINTINGS	Caroline Cook	186
WALL APPENDAGES	Caroline Cook	188
WINDOWS including TRACERY	Paul Vincent	189
WOODWORK	Caroline Cook	200
GUIDE TO ENGLISH PERIODS AND STYLES FOR ALL SECTIONS		236
APPENDIX – MOULDINGS		237
INDEX		238

PREFACE

'But how do we start?'

'Break it up!'

Agonised gasp from hovering incumbent.

Giggles from group of new recorders.

'No, break it down - no - do it piece by piece - for instance this is the ....' - the word 'cornice' floated out of my mind to get entangled among the fronds of the green-man corbel leering down at us. I realised that NADFAS must have a handbook in which every part and term was illustrated.

Nearly every object has a top, middle and bottom, but the correct terminology for those of a column are 'capital', 'shaft' and 'base' (and I wasn't then quite sure of the difference between a column and a pillar). It also sounds more professional to describe a boy on a cow as 'an immortal on an ox' - St Luke's symbol is also an 'ox', not a cow or a bull! The top of a chalice is a 'bowl', the middle is the 'stem' and the bottom is the 'foot' which sometimes has a 'base'. There are accepted names for all the other bits and pieces, such as calyx, toe, knop or knot, bouge, rim, etc., and one learns that pewter and ceramics have their own peculiar terms.

During the course of research for this guide, the author found so many words to describe the same object or type of decoration, and that different experts had their own favourite terms, that it became impracticable to give every alternative, therefore in most cases only one term has been given, but readers should feel at liberty to use the word they remember most easily and if no word springs to mind, those used in this guide will not, it is hoped, be wrong. The only wrong term is one that is mis-applied and if there is doubt a dictionary should be consulted. It is of help to others if the name of the glossary used is mentioned in the recording.

Every effort has been made to put the correct terms adjacent to the illustrations and to cover most of the furnishings of a church. The sample descriptions fall where most convenient, usually alphabetically in the sections, and are shown by a * in the index; but

it will be found necessary for, say someone describing a piece of
furniture to consult not only the woodwork section but also those on
architecture, decoration, framework, etc., and to refer to the index
for examples of each part of the object. The index is a very important part of the guide.

To have dated everything would have required many more illustrations to cover every overlapping period, therefore in many cases
dates are not given. Sizes and woods have also mostly been omitted,
to save space, as it is assumed that readers will know that it is of
the utmost importance to give such details. Only occasional
reference is made to style as one or two illustrations of each would
be inadequate.

Bibliographies are attached to each section, even if it has meant
much repetition of the same works, because, from experience, the
compiler realised that someone describing something of one material
might not always think of looking at the books mentioned in other
sections. Acknowledgment is here made of the use of text and illustrations from all the books mentioned - books which are available in
most public libraries. Specialist material, listed in the 'Antiques
Reference Book' compiled by A.W. Coysh and J. King (David & Charles,
Newton Abbot) is not available to all and often does not fulfil the
needs of those for whom this book is intended, e.g. those who want
to know how to describe something.

Members of the staff of the Victoria & Albert Museum have, from
the start when Mr Charles Gibbs-Smith suggested that the work should
be published rather than duplicated, right through all the months of
preparation, been most helpful, especially

Mr John Physick, Keeper of Museum Services,
Dr Charles Avery and Mr Leonard Joyce, Department of Architecture
    and Sculpture,
Mr Michael Archer, Department of Ceramics,
Mr Simon Jervis, Department of Furniture and Woodwork,
Mr Claude Blair, Mrs Shirley Bury, Mr John Cooper and Miss Somers
    Cocks, Department of Metalwork,
Mr Donald King and Miss Levey, Department of Textiles.

We have continually made use of illustrations and descriptions
from the Museum's catalogue of the Victorian Church Art exhibition
of 1971-2, which no recorder should be without.

I would also like to thank Mr Anthony Wells-Cole of Temple Newsam
House and Mr Miller of Wipple Mowbray Church Furnishing Ltd for pro-
viding us with catalogues and for their help. Publishers and
authors, mentioned in the bibliographies, have been most generous
and co-operative and everyone at Routledge & Kegan Paul has shown
much interest.

We would like to tell members of NADFAS, who have kept us going
with their enthusiasm about the project when they could so easily
have dampened our spirits, that we are sorry to have kept them wait-
ing so long - but it has become a question of 'How do we stop?'

P.D.
C.C.
F.C.
P.V.

HOW TO USE THE GUIDE

If the name of the object to be described is not known look through
the book to find an illustration, trying first the section dealing
with the material and remembering that much the same terminology is
used for all.

Having found the name, consult the INDEX to see if there is a
sample description (marked with an *) and compare with the object to
be described.

For example to describe a metal jug with a lid - the flagons on
pp.122, 123, 124 would be the nearest. To ascertain whether it is
silver or other metal, consult the INDEX under 'metals'. If it is
silver describe the marks (by consulting the INDEX for 'marks'),
give the details required which will be found at the beginning of
the metalwork section, i.e. measurements, weight, etc.

Give a general idea of the shape by consulting the section on
SHAPES and then break the object down into parts, from the top if
most convenient, and proceed to describe the shapes, decoration and
techniques employed for those various parts.

There is a section on decoration and the techniques for various
materials will be found by consulting the INDEX for 'techniques'.

To find the names of parts, some being common to more than one,
others peculiar to certain materials, will necessitate consulting
the INDEX and perhaps looking up all the references - e.g. legs and
certain feet mostly used in woodwork are placed in that section, but
the same name or term will be used should the leg or foot be of
metal.

The lettering of an inscription or text will be found under
'lettering', but the way the lettering is worked will be under the
'techniques' for the particular material in the INDEX.

Architectural terms should be used wherever possible.

The term 'COLUMN' describes any one of the five Classical ORDERS.
Supports deviating in shape from the Orders have other names.
Greek and Roman Orders differ slightly.

DORIC   distinguished by triglyphs and metopes in the frieze and
        mutules under the corona. Greek Doric has a fluted shaft and
        no base. Roman Doric has a base and fluted or plain shaft.

IONIC   has volutes on the capital and dentils in the cornice; the
        shaft is usually fluted and the base 'Attic'.

CORINTHIAN normally has a fluted shaft and the capital ornamented
        with Acanthus, Olive or Laurel and eight small volutes.

TUSCAN is a simplified Doric.

COMPOSITE is an ornate version of Corinthian and occurs in various
        forms.

Doric   Ionic   Corinthian   Tuscan   Composite

Other Capitals

Cushion
Norman

Scalloped
Norman

Waterleaf
12th century

Stiff Leaf
13th century

Natural
Leaf
14th century

Crocket or
Volute
Transitional

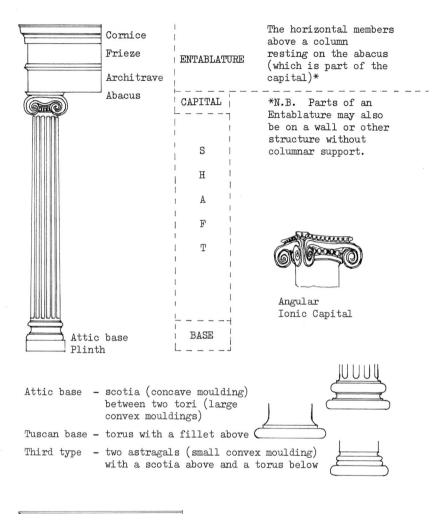

Cornice

Frieze

Architrave

Abacus

ENTABLATURE

The horizontal members above a column resting on the abacus (which is part of the capital)*

CAPITAL

S

H

A

F

T

*N.B. Parts of an Entablature may also be on a wall or other structure without columnar support.

Angular
Ionic Capital

Attic base
Plinth

BASE

Attic base – scotia (concave moulding) between two tori (large convex mouldings)

Tuscan base – torus with a fillet above

Third type – two astragals (small convex moulding) with a scotia above and a torus below

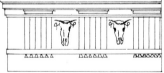

Doric frieze with mutules (projecting brackets) above triglyphs (grooved tablets) alternating with metopes (square spaces) and with guttae (drops) below

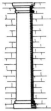

Engaged Column

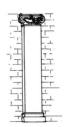

Pilaster
(rectangular)

(support
projecting
slightly from
a surface,
with base and
capital)

Colonnettes
(diminutive columns)

Pilarettes or
Pilasterettes
(diminutive)

Pier or Pillar
(a solid detached upright
support, deviating in shape
and proportion from the
Orders)

Lesene or
Pilaster Strip

(a pilaster
without base
or capital)

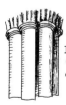

Pillar of clustered shafts
(often misnamed as a
clustered column)

Compound Pier

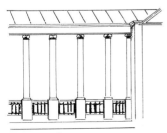

Colonnade

Blind
Arcade

SAXON 7th century - 1066
Round shafts. Few and very plain mouldings.
Massive impost blocks.

NORMAN 1066-1200
Some plain mouldings, but many richly carved,
their chief characteristic being a series of
concentric rings, each one projecting more
than the one under it. Beakheads and chevron
popular motifs. Abacus square-edged on top.
Capitals cushioned, scalloped or volute.

The Lancet arch appeared during
this period.

EARLY ENGLISH (Gothic) 1200-1300
Mouldings of deeply cut rounds and hollows.
Rounded Abacus. Dogtooth and stiff leaf
ornament. Shafts round and at times
clustered. Arches acutely pointed or
trefoil.
(For Foils and Cusps see WINDOWS section.)

DECORATED (Gothic) 1300-50
Numerous lightly cut mouldings.
Ogee curves. Abacus absorbed into capital
and composed of three members with ornament
between rolls of moulding. Crockets and
pinnacles abound.

PERPENDICULAR (Gothic) 1350-1660
Arches less pointed, some segmental or flat
headed. Mouldings wide and shallow and
sometimes carried right round the arch down
to the floor.
Ornament of scroll, ballflower, fourleaf and
naturalistic foliage, Tudor rose and Tudor
flower and much brattishing.

RENAISSANCE 1603-89 - CLASSICAL 1689-1837
Style based on the Antique Classical Orders
with round arch and piers.
Cherubs and garlands incorporated in the decoration.

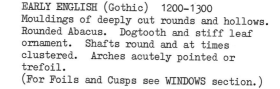

PEDIMENT
An ornamental low pitched
triangular or segmental gable
above the cornice of an
entablature.

Triangular   Segmental

Broken   Open   Scrolled   Swan-necked

CORNICE
The projecting member below a pediment,
or the uppermost member of an entablature,
surmounting the frieze, or any moulded
projection which crowns the part to which
it is fixed, e.g. wall, door, column,
piece of furniture, window, panelling, etc.

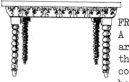

FRIEZE
A decorative band or feature between the
architrave and cornice, or in furniture between
the cornice and the framework - it sometimes
covers the top rail. On a wall, it is the
band between the cornice and the rest.

ARCHITRAVE
The moulded frame surrounding a door or window.
It is also the lowest main division of the entablature,
between the frieze and abacus.
A LINTEL is the horizontal member over a door or window.

ABACUS
The slab on top of a capital on which the architrave
rests; the shape varies according to the Order.

IMPOST
The slab, usually moulded, on which the ends of
an arch rest.

SPUR
An ornamental protrusion on the corner between
the base of a column or pillar and the plinth.
Also a fixed draught screen, or a buttress.

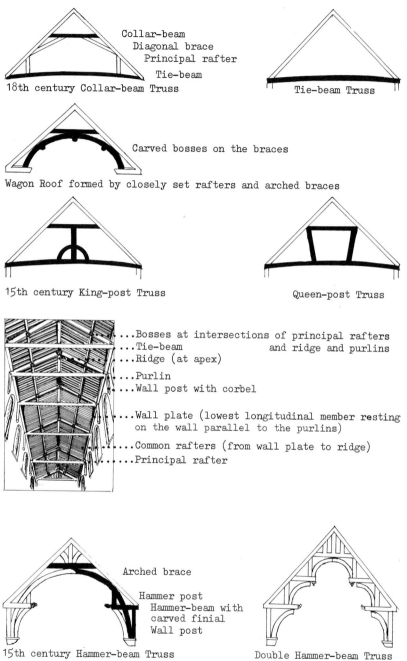

Collar-beam
Diagonal brace
Principal rafter
Tie-beam

18th century Collar-beam Truss

Tie-beam Truss

Carved bosses on the braces

Wagon Roof formed by closely set rafters and arched braces

15th century King-post Truss

Queen-post Truss

...Bosses at intersections of principal rafters
...Tie-beam   and ridge and purlins
...Ridge (at apex)
...Purlin
...Wall post with corbel

...Wall plate (lowest longitudinal member resting
   on the wall parallel to the purlins)
...Common rafters (from wall plate to ridge)
...Principal rafter

Arched brace

Hammer post
Hammer-beam with
   carved finial
Wall post

15th century Hammer-beam Truss

Double Hammer-beam Truss

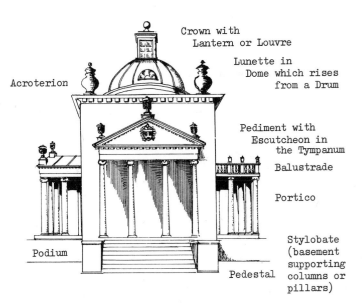

Crown with
Lantern or Louvre

Lunette in
Dome which rises
from a Drum

Acroterion

Pediment with
Escutcheon in
the Tympanum

Balustrade

Portico

Stylobate
(basement
supporting
Pedestal columns or
pillars)

Pedestal

Podium

TYMPANUM
the filled-in
space of a
pediment or of
the curved section
of an arch

LUNETTE
semi-circular
window, panel or
decoration

LUCARNE
on a spire

EYE, OCULUS or
OEIL-de-BOEUF
round or oval
window with
radiating glazing
bars, not to be
confused with a

DORMER
on a house roof

ORIEL
when supported
on corbels

WHEEL or ROSE
window which
has concentric
or radiating
tracery

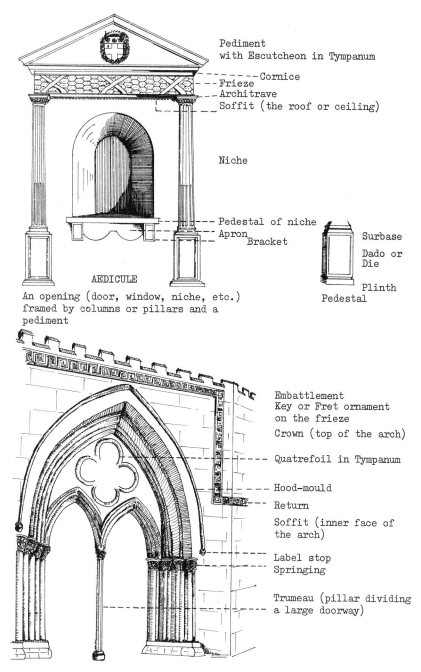

Pediment
with Escutcheon in Tympanum

Cornice
Frieze
Architrave
Soffit (the roof or ceiling)

Niche

Pedestal of niche
Apron
Bracket

Surbase

Dado or
Die

Plinth

Pedestal

AEDICULE
An opening (door, window, niche, etc.)
framed by columns or pillars and a
pediment

Embattlement
Key or Fret ornament
on the frieze

Crown (top of the arch)

Quatrefoil in Tympanum

Hood-mould

Return

Soffit (inner face of
the arch)

Label stop
Springing

Trumeau (pillar dividing
a large doorway)

Hatchment in Spandrel
of nave arcade

Respond
a half pillar or
shaft engaged in
a wall to support
an arch, usually
at the end of an
arcade

ARCADE a series of arches supported on piers or columns.
N.B. in the above illustration the dado rail is 'returned',
i.e. branching at right angles.

BIBLIOGRAPHY

CHILD, M. (1976), 'Discovering Church Architecture', Shire
Publications, Aylesbury.
HARRIES, J. (1972), 'Discovering Churches', Shire Publications,
Aylesbury.
HARRIS, J. and LEVER, J. (1966), 'Illustrated Glossary of Architec-
ture 850-1830', Faber & Faber, London.
JONES, L.E. (1965), 'The Observer's Book of Old English Churches',
Warne, London.
PEVSNER, N., Buildings of England Series, Penguin, Harmondsworth.
THE ROYAL COMMISSION ON HISTORICAL MONUMENTS.

Most church documents are now deposited in the county record
offices, where enquirers can usually get a list and permission to
view, but the Church Chest, Vestry, Belfry, Rectory and elsewhere
should also be searched.

REGISTERS record Births or Baptisms, Marriages, Banns and Deaths:
they are often mixed together.

Vestry and PCC Minutes are a source of information.

Visitors' Books, Registers of Services, Gift Books, War Memorial
Books, Village Histories, Bibles, Prayer Books, Music and the Church
Library of ecclesiastical works, Church Leaflets and Parish
Magazines, are amongst the works that should be looked for.

A MISSAL is the term for the Service Book for the use of the priest.

A FACULTY is an authorisation from the Diocesan Office for some
alteration or addition to the church and usually the names of the
architect, designer, donor, material, as well as the date, are given.
Every effort should be made to locate FACULTIES.

A TERRIER is an inventory of Church possessions: it should be
consulted and checked.

The essential information required for the description of a book
or document is the Title, Author, Illustrator, Publisher, Date, Size,
Binding, Inscriptions and other marks.

TERMINOLOGY

Back	Spine of book.
Bands	Ridges on spine caused by the sewing cords.
Binding	Outside cover.
Blind tooled	Impressions, without gold infill, made with tools.
Boards	Sides of bound or cased book.
Bolts	Folds which have to be cut before page can be read.
Cancels	Pages containing errors and the corrected pages.
Cartouche	Used loosely in bookbinding for round, oval or decorated labels.
Colophon	In old books the tail-piece, often ornamental: now placed on title-page.
Deckle	Rough natural edge of hand-made paper.
Dentelle	Border with lacy pattern on inner edge.
Doublure	Endpapers of leather.
Endpapers	Folded leaves, pasted down, at the front and back.
Fillet	A ruled tooled line on the cover.
Finishing	The lettering and decoration.
Fly-leaf	Blank page at the beginning or end.
Fore-edge	Front edge. 'Fore-edge paintings' show when book is opened.
French grooves	Deep concave joints between spine and boards.
Format	Size and shape.
Gauffering	Gilt edges decorated with finishing tools.
Guards	Folded strips of paper sewn or pasted into the back.
Gutter	The spine margin.

Head and Tail	Top and bottom of spine.
Headband	Ornamental beading sometimes worked in silk thread, at head and tail.
Headcap	Leather at top and tail of spine, drawn out to cover the headband.
Hollow	The spine of a cased book.
Label (skiver)	Thin pieces of morocco (even on a calf book) with lettering. From 1750 Paper labels were applied to paper spines.
Manuscript	(MS. in sing., MSS. in pl.) Book or Document written by hand.
Marbling	The process of colouring paper or edges to imitate marble.
Panel	Rectangle formed of single or multiple fillets, gilt or blind, on boards or between bands on spine.
Panel stamped	Leather bindings decorated in blind with engraved blocks.
Plate	An illustration printed on different paper from the text.
Recto/Verso	Right-hand page/Left-hand page.
Repairs	Books may be Re-backed, Re-joined, Re-margined, Remboitaged, Re-set.
Semis	Repeating pattern made with small tools (semé).
Sprinkled	Small specks on edges of leaves or on calf bindings, usually dull red.
Stamp	Impressed pattern.
t.e.g.	Top edge gilt.
Title-page	Page at beginning giving particulars of subject, authorship, publication, etc.
Tail-piece	Decorative finish at the end of a chapter or of a book.
Tooling	Decoration of cover by hand tools.
Uncut	Not to be confused with 'Unopened' (see Bolts). Edges not having been cut down by a rebinder.
Watermark	Mark on paper visible when held to light.

Whole Bound

Half Bound

Quarter Bound

Three-quarter Bound

Yapp Binding

Cased Book

A Wrappered Book is a paper-back, not a book with a dust-wrapper

Calf	Smooth, without grain, can be variously treated and coloured.
Forel	Parchment dressed to look like vellum.
Morocco	Goatskin - grained.
Parchment	Usually sheep or goat, prepared for writing or painting.
Russia Leather	Rich and smooth cowhide, richly scented, often decorated with blind lozenge pattern.
Spanish Calf	Bold dashes of red and green acid on calf binding.
Tree Calf	A calf binding with the sides stained to resemble a tree.
Vellum	Very fine parchment - calf.

Armorial	Binding stamped with coat of arms, which may have been added at a later date. Royal arms do not necessarily denote royal ownership, not even if there is a dedication to a royal personage.
Cathedral Binding	Gothic architectural decoration often including a rose window - 1810-40.
Cottage Binding	A gable discernible at top and bottom in the decoration - 1660-1770.
Dos à dos	Two volumes bound back to back with a common lower board.
Fanfare style	Decoration of interlacement.
Etruscan	Classical decoration.
Irish	A paper lozenge label in centre of board.
Mosaic	Polychrome decoration of binding by use of paint, onlays or inlays.
Publishers Cloth	Original uniform bindings dating from 1823, becoming collectors' pieces.
Rococo	C-shaped curves and shells date in bookbinding from late 1770s and 1780s.
Scots Binding	Recognisable by wheel pattern.
Sombre Bindings	Black leather, tooled in blind - popular 1675-1725.
Vulcanite	Bindings stiff and hard, the leaves liable to drop out.

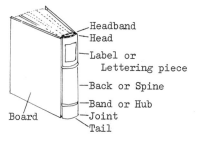

Headband
Head
Label or Lettering piece
Back or Spine
Band or Hub
Board
Joint
Tail

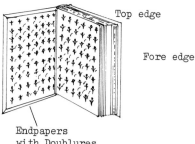

Top edge

Fore edge

Endpapers with Doublures
All three exposed edges fully clad in gold

Association Copy	Term applied to a copy which is associated by ownership or annotation with the author, or with someone in connection with the author or the contents, or with someone of interest in his own right.
Beau Livre	Usually of limited edition, with original illustrations and embellishments.
Dedication Copy	Presented by the author to the person to whom the book is dedicated.
Inscribed Copy	Autographed by the author, usually at the request of the owner.
Limited Edition	Usually individually numbered.
Mint Condition	Good as new.
N. d.	No date on title-page.
Presentation Copy	A spontaneous gift of the author - in this case the value lies in the interest of, or the connection with the author, of the recipient.
Provenance	The pedigree of a book's previous ownership.
Signed Binding	Attributed by the 'binder's ticket', a printed or engraved label, or by the name letter stamped inside the front or back cover or at the foot of the spine, or in ink at the edge of one of the end papers, known as 'name pallets' or by an MS. note of the owner for whom it was bound.
Folio	Leaf of paper folded once, usually more than 45 cm high.
Octavo (8vo)	Leaf of paper folded three times, i.e. into eight, usually between 15 and 25 cm high.
Quarto (4to)	Leaf of paper folded twice, i.e. into four, usually between 25 and 40 cm high.
Horae or Book of Hours	Manuscript or printed collection of prayers for private use.
Horn-book	Matter used for the teaching of children, 16th-18th centuries, on a leaf of paper protected by a thin plate of translucent horn and mounted on a wooden tablet with handle. (N.B. It might be possible to find such a tablet in use holding a church guide.)

ABBREVIATIONS

A.l.	Autographed letter	A.l.s.	Signed autographed letter
A.n.	Autographed note	A.n.s.	Signed autographed note
A.D.	Autographed document	A.d.s.	Signed autographed document

The above refer to letters, notes or fragments and documents in the hand of the writer, either signed or not signed. When the 'A' is omitted the material is probably in a clerk's hand.

BIBLIOGRAPHY

'Cassell's Dictionary of Abbreviations' (1966), Cassell, London.
DARLEY, L.S. (1906), 'Introduction to Book Binding', Faber & Faber,
London.
DAVENPORT, C.J.H. (1910), 'Encyclopaedia Britannica', 11th ed.
RAMSEY, L.G.G. (1962), 'The Complete Encyclopaedia of Antiques', The
Connoisseur, London (extensive glossary).
VICTORIA & ALBERT MUSEUM (1971), Catalogue of 'Victorian Church
Art'.

When giving a REFERENCE there are differences of preference:
The Victoria & Albert Museum like to have the following format
for a book:

A.N. AUTHOR, <u>Title of Book</u>, Publisher, Town, Date;

for an article in a journal:

A.N. AUTHOR, 'Title of article', <u>Title of Journal</u>, vol.xxx, 1976,
pp.39-41;

for information taken from a Church Leaflet:

<u>Name and Place of Church</u>, nth edition, 1977.

It will be noted, that as the work in hand is a 'DIRECT EDITION'
the Publishers prefer a different arrangement which does not
necessitate underlining, e.g.

AUTHOR, A.N. (1977), 'Title of Book', Publisher.

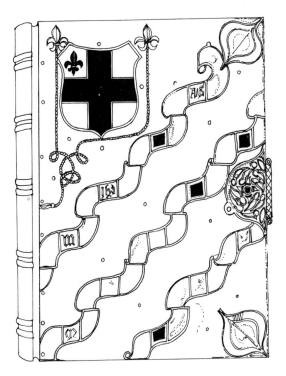

The New Testament.   Published by ..... 1894.
37.5 x 30 cm   Bound by .... (label on back endpaper)
                      Enamels executed by ..... (ref. V. & A.
                      catalogue of 'Victorian Church Art', 1971, 0.3)

Red leather binding with silver panels on both covers.

Upper cover: three bands of spiralling ribbon decoration with
moulded edges and set with enamels bearing sacred monograms
on copper (all much worn), descending diagonally from R to L.
In top L corner an enamelled shield with coat of arms,
(arg. a cross gu. in dexter chief a fleur-de-lys az. for .....),
surrounded by rope moulding with fleur-de-lys finials flanking
the shield at the top.
Raised lobed bosses at top and bottom R corners.

Lower cover: eight inset enamels on copper.
In top R corner an enamelled swan with motto (.....) below,
surrounded by rope moulding.
Raised lobed bosses at top and bottom L corners.

Brass clasp with a roundel of mouchette tracery on the upper cover.

G.E. STREET, 'The Cathedral of the Holy Trinity commonly called
Christ Church Cathedral, Dublin. An account of the restoration of
the fabric', Sutton Sharpe & Co., London, 1882. (V. & A. cat. E.14.)

48.5 x 34.5 cm. Bound by Burn & Co. (label on back endpaper)

White vellum with panel stamps in gold and red.

Three rectangular borders, the innermost with repeated monogram CC
between leafy sprays.

In centre panel, 19th century Lombardic lettering, 'Christ Church
Cathedral' at top and 'Dublin' at foot. At the intersection of a
cross, the seal of the cathedral; at the head and foot of the cross,
the arms of the archbishop and of the founder (Loftus?). Between the
arms, reticulated ornament of trefoil cusped ogival compartments with
a shamrock in each centre: the corners filled with a leafy spray.

Information required:

1 Position in church.

2 Component parts, noting whether relaid or palimpsest,
   parts missing and if they are to be found elsewhere,
   repairs. Note whether any enamelling remains. Measurements.

3 Description (see also sections on COSTUME and VESTMENTS)
   using recognised abbreviations.

4 Description of canopy or border.

5 Heraldry - blazon unless well-known.

6 Inscription in full.

7 Describe any Merchants' Marks which may be found on shell-
   shaped plates, roundels, in canopies, in marginal
   inscriptions, and are sometimes based on religious or
   secular symbols, initials, cyphers, etc.

8 Casements with Indents from missing brasses should also be
   recorded.

ABBREVIATIONS

acad.	- academical dress	mutil.	- mutilated
arm.	- dressed in armour	pr.	- priest
civ.	- in civilian dress	qd.pl.	- quadrangular plate
dau.	- daughter	R.	- re-used (palimpsest)
demi	- half effigy	sm.	- small (less than 45 cm)
fem.	- female	w.	- wife
frag.	- fragment	B.C.L.	- iuris canonici baccalaureus
inscr.	- inscription	LL.B.	- in utroque iure baccalaureus
kng	- kneeling	S.T.B.	- sacrae theologiae baccalaureus
knt	- knight	S.T.P.	- sacrae theologiae professor
marg.	- marginal	S.T.S.	- sacrae theologiae scholaris
mur.	- mural	vv.	- verses

All Orders of Clergy received the tonsure and wore the same dress
except the sexton. Some had a symbol such as:

Acolyte - a candle
Doorkeeper (sexton) - a key
Exorcist - a holy water pot
Lector - a book
Sub-deacon - a basin and ewer

Palimpsest is the term applied to re-used brasses, mostly of the 16th
century. For details of five types of changes see Macklin's
'Monumental Brasses'.

Shrouded figures and skeletons date from mid 15th century to end of
16th century.

LETTERING

13th and early 14th centuries - Lombardic Uncials: each letter set in
    its own matrix around the border of the casement, in most cases
    only indents remain: Norman French with phonetic spelling.
14th century - Early Old English or Black Letter (round): marginal
    inscriptions on fillets (strips), sometimes a second plate
    added below the figures: Latin with abbreviations.
15th century - Straight Old English (difficult to read, letters
    composed of straight lines): precatory scrolls (or labels)
    issuing from hands and mouths, also foot inscriptions.
16th century - Tudor - more fanciful.
17th century - Roman capitals and some examples of Rough Script:
    rectangular plates.
18th century - Roman caps and smalls, Script, Italic and mid 18th
    century Gothick lettering: plates with decorative borders.
(See section on LETTERING.)

The dialect and spelling of the Early English inscriptions is mainly
that of Chaucer and many begin and end with the same phrases, viz:
'Of your charity pray for the soul of ...' and 'On whose soul Jesus
have mercy. Amen.'

    Terminations are often cut off; 'm' and 'n' omitted; a dash
above a letter indicating omissions: 'p' stands for per, pro or prae
and 'xps' for Christus.

    Some of the more common archaic words:

Miles	- Knight	Dominus	- Master
Generosus	- Gentleman	Decanus	- Dean
Gent	- Gentleman or	Capellanus	- Chaplain
	Gentlewoman	Prepositus	- Provost
Armiger	- Esquire	Elemosinarius	- Almoner
Comes	- Earl	Pannarius	- Draper
Consul	- Counsellor	Pelliparius	- Tanner

almys	- alms	mede	- merit
auncynt	- ancient	moder	- mother
aungeles	- angels	or	- our
awtere	- altar	pish	- parish
bles	- bliss	pson	- parson
certes	- surely	quere	- choir or chancel
cheyffe	- chief	redecion	- redemption
crysten	- christian	sowlys	- souls
deptyd	- departed	steven	- staves of music
eke	- also	s'teyne	- certain
erchdiakn	- archdeacon	thred	- third
eyre	- heir	twey	- two
fadyr	- father	vestment	- a set of vestments
ffro	- from	wen	- think
halud	- hallowed	whylom	- once
hem	- them	wot	- know
maden	- made	yat/ys	- that/this
mci	- mercy	yistis	- gifts

The following is only a very small sample of arms and armour. There
is no need to mention every part when describing brasses, but it
is useful to know the names in case parts are missing and also for
dating if the inscription is not clear.

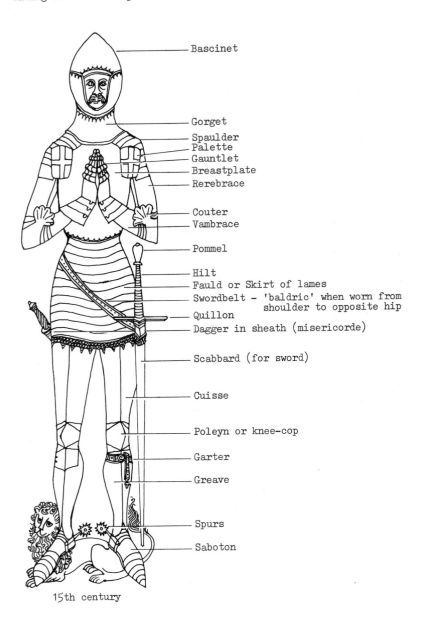

Bascinet

Gorget

Spaulder
Palette
Gauntlet
Breastplate
Rerebrace

Couter
Vambrace

Pommel

Hilt
Fauld or Skirt of lames
Swordbelt - 'baldric' when worn from
            shoulder to opposite hip
Quillon
Dagger in sheath (misericorde)

Scabbard (for sword)

Cuisse

Poleyn or knee-cop

Garter

Greave

Spurs

Saboton

15th century

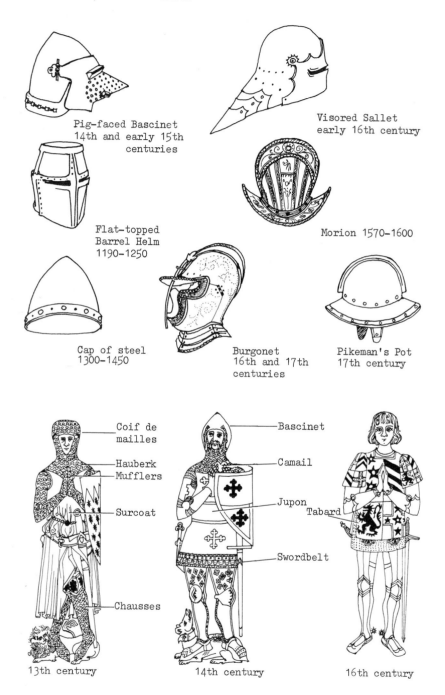

Pig-faced Bascinet
14th and early 15th
centuries

Visored Sallet
early 16th century

Flat-topped
Barrel Helm
1190-1250

Morion 1570-1600

Cap of steel
1300-1450

Burgonet
16th and 17th
centuries

Pikeman's Pot
17th century

Coif de
mailles

Haubergk
Mufflers

Surcoat

Chausses

13th century

Bascinet

Camail

Jupon

Swordbelt

14th century

Tabard

16th century

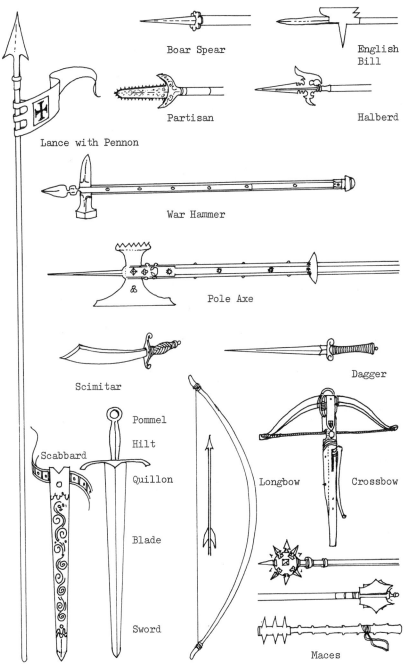

Boar Spear

English Bill

Partisan

Halberd

Lance with Pennon

War Hammer

Pole Axe

Scimitar

Dagger

Pommel

Hilt

Scabbard

Quillon

Longbow

Crossbow

Blade

Sword

Maces

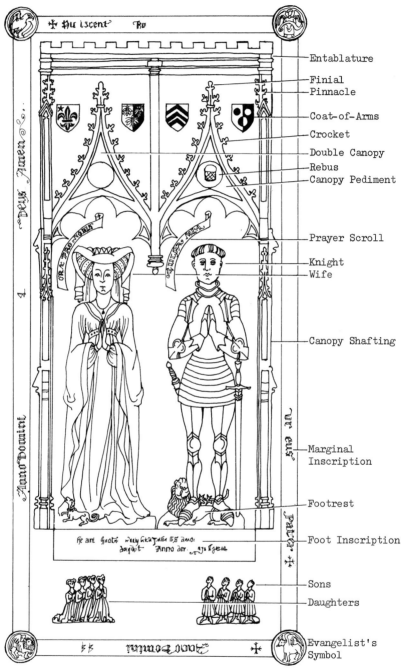

Entablature

Finial
Pinnacle

Coat-of-Arms

Crocket

Double Canopy

Rebus
Canopy Pediment

Prayer Scroll

Knight
Wife

Canopy Shafting

Marginal
Inscription

Footrest

Foot Inscription

Sons
Daughters

Evangelist's
Symbol

1443 Sir William Colwell, w. & ch.

1 Floor, centre of S Aisle. 94 x 44 cm overall.

2 Two figures each 40 cm h.
Group of four daus below w. and four sons below knt.

Four shields of arms flanking canopy pinnacles.

Latin Black Letter marginal inscr. (worn), foot inscr.
of two lines and prayer scrolls.

Traces of enamelling on sword hilt and in shields.

3 Bare-headed knt on R in 15th century plate armour with hands
conjoined, lion footrest, rowel spurs, skirt of lames,
sword and dagger, no visible swordbelt.

W. wears wide horned headdress and houpelande: dog at foot.

4 Crocketed and pinnacled double canopy with embattled entablature
and pinnacled shafting.

Evangelists' symbols in roundels at corners of margin.

5 Arms in shields, from L to R

1 Arg. a fleur-de-lys sa. in dexter chief a mullet vert (Gayre)

2 Per pale az. and gu. three gadflies or (Dorre)

3 Arg. three chevrons sa. (Colwell)

4 Per pale or and gu. three roundels counterchanged (D'Abetot)

6 Inscr. in margin ....

Inscr. at foot ....

Prayer in L label ....

Prayer in R label ....

7 Rebus in roundel in canopy above knt's head, 'a collet above a
well'.

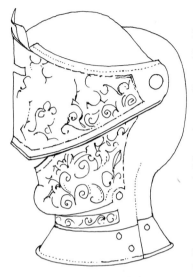

FUNERAL HELMET

put together by an Undertaker
and possibly incorporating bits
and pieces of genuine helmets.
Genuine helmets have a mark on
the back, sometimes overpainted.

Armour over tombs, although
usually a mixed lot, should be
studied, as it is possible to find a
genuine piece. Some may be over the
wrong tombs owing to mistakes by
undertakers and others.

Genuine armour and firearms were
stored in churches.

There are lists of known church
armour in the Victoria & Albert
Museum, London (C.F. Laking, vol.V
and supplement by F.H. Cripps-Day
1939).

BIBLIOGRAPHY

BLAIR, CLAUDE (1958), 'European Armour circa 1066 to circa 1700',
Batsford, London.
COOK, M. (1971), 'Discovering Brasses and Brass Rubbing', Shire
Publications, Aylesbury.
MACKLIN, H.W. (1905), 'Monumental Brasses', rev. J.P. PHILLIPS
(1975), Allen & Unwin, London.
MANN, SIR JAMES (1969), rev. A.R. DUFFY, 'An Outline of Arms and
Armour in England', HMSO, London.
MILL STEPHENSON, B.A. (1926), 'A List of Monumental Brasses in the
British Isles', Headley, London.
OXFORD UNIVERSITY ARCHAEOLOGICAL SOCIETY (1973), 'Notes on Brass
Rubbing', Ashmolean Museum, Oxford.
RAMSEY, L.G.G. (1962), 'The Complete Encyclopaedia of Antiques', The
Connoisseur, London.
TRIVICK, H. (1971), 'The Picture Book of Brasses in Gilt', John
Baker, London.
UDEN, GRANT (1968), 'A Dictionary of Chivalry', Longmans, London.

Church recorders may possibly find a piece of mediaeval pottery that has been appropriated by a flower arranger, or a container of value that has been lent or donated - even a cracked mid 18th century piece has become a desirable collectors' item. For amateurs a reference book is essential.

A brief and useful guide is 'The Country Life Collectors' Pocket Book' by G. Bernard Hughes, in which the different WARES are described, the forms and methods of decoration, the accepted terminology, and some MARKS are illustrated.

Any object with a MARK (the sign of origin applied usually on the base in either underglaze blue, impressed, incised or painted above the glaze) should be recorded with a photograph or drawing and a note of the shape, glaze, colour and design. Technical details are more important than factory trademarks which can be forgeries or legitimate imitations - i.e. WORCESTER not only used their own, but also the personal marks of their master-potters, oriental marks and even those of Meissen, Sèvres, Tournay, Chantilly and others. 'Flight', 'Barr' and 'Chamberlain' are names used by Worcester between 1783 and c.1840.

Between 1842 and 1883 a Registration Mark was used by many factories to protect a design from copying by rivals, the marks changing as with silver.

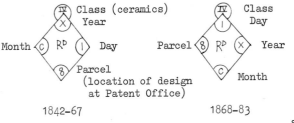

An item marked 'Made in England' dates from the late 19th century.

Anything hand painted, unless obviously amateurish, is of interest.

Any Pottery or Porcelain with an UNDERGLAZE blue print, even if not marked, should be recorded. Recorders who do not recognise UNDERGLAZE would benefit by being shown a piece.

Porcelain is TRANSLUCENT, the body is always white and almost invariably has a transparent glaze, which may be slightly blued. Vases are glazed inside and out, as it is part of the basic firing process.

Pottery is OPAQUE, the clay body varying from brown, grey, red, orange to white. When the body is not white, and it is wished to imitate porcelain, a white opaque glaze is used. Pottery being porous, has to be glazed, at least on the inside, if it is to hold liquid.

The following MARKS could be of interest:

Meissen, either genuine or imitation.

possibly Bow, Chelsea, Derby, Venice, or 19th century copies.

WEDGWOOD note the full mark, lettering AND spelling, as
other firms used the name.
WEDGEWOOD would not be genuine.

(C   could be 18th century English soft paste.

SPODE GARRETT COPELAND DOULTON all names of interest.

and similar marks in red, blue or purple, or incised,
could be Derby c.1785-1830.

Typical 'Fancy' outline used by Victorian
factories - name of pattern usually written
and pattern number often included.

It is often possible to date or attribute a porcelain jug by
comparing the shape with contemporary silver - i.e. a tall helmet-
shaped silver jug would not have been designed until around 1775,
therefore a porcelain jug of this style would have to coincide or
follow this date - see sections on METALWORK and SHAPES.

18th century 'Sparrow beak' jug, from 8 to 23 cm
h. May be ribbed or plain.
The ceramic term for a handle terminal or finial
is 'kick back', and for the protrusion on top of
a cover is 'knop' (rather than finial).

Mid 19th century Dragon Vase
with six-character mark of
K'ang Hsi.

Globular body and cylindrical
neck, decorated with nine
scaly five-clawed dragons,
all of different colour and
with ferocious expressions,
on a ground of white crested
waves painted in underglaze-
blue. 54.6 cm h. (sample
description)

Although copies of Roman mosaic pavements (tesserae) exist (where the design is produced by the outline of individual pieces of tiles), and 12th century pavements such as those in Canterbury (where stone tiles are engraved with pictorial designs and the sunken parts filled with dark cement), English pavements were usually laid with ENCAUSTIC floor tiles. They were mostly produced by monastic potters from the early 13th to 16th centuries, the skill dying with the closing of the monasteries.

Tiles about 4 cm thick and 11 cm square were made of native red-brick earths and white pipe-clays, producing a yellowish-white pattern relieved against red or chocolate and glazed with natural lead glaze. When worn, the background falls away, leaving the inlay in relief.

The design, either a single unit or one of a group of four, or a combination of tiles forming a cross as found on mortuary slabs, enables the place of manufacture to be identified. In some counties designs have been recorded and numbered and NADFAS members should refer to the published reference.

During the 17th and 18th centuries tiles, or the workmen to make them, came from abroad and the ware was too soft for use as floor pavements which were replaced by common buff or red terracotta quarry tiles.

From 1830 the Gothic Revival brought new interest and firms such as Minton, Maw and Godwin produced mechanically made tiles to designs based on old work, even incorporating the 'faults'; although usually with a red clay body and white figure, they were sometimes in black and buff. From about 1860 other colours were introduced and the size gradually increased to about 16 cm square.

Although examples of encaustic tiles used as reredos are found, most wall tiles will be of softer paste and foreign workmanship until the mid 19th century.

DELFTWARE	blue and white soft tiles made in England and Holland from 17th century.
ENCAUSTIC	made of red clay, the pattern stamped in by a wooden die while the clay is still wet, then filled with a white clay, covered with yellow glaze and fired in a furnace.
GROUND	body of tile as opposed to decorative part.
INCISED	cut into surface.
INTAGLIO	indented pattern - opposite of relief.
MAJOLICA	Italian and Spanish painted and lustred tiles, usually square or hexagonal and of soft paste - also 19th century copies of same.
QUARRIES	plain one-coloured square or diamond shaped tiles.
TESSERAE or TESSELATED PAVEMENT	decorative floor or wall mosaic made up of small blocks of stone, marble, tile, earthenware, etc. and embedded in cement.

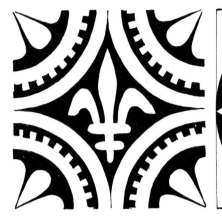

Fleur-de-lys between four
quadrants, each enclosing an
embattled quadrant and a quarter
octofoil. (Penn, 44 in 'Records
of Buckinghamshire', vol.XIV)

Design based on the Solomon's Seal
with a quatrefoil at the centre
within a star. (Penn, 93)

Part of a four-tile design of
formal foliage in a quatrefoil,
with foliage and fleurs-de-lys
cut by a quadrant in the outer
angles. Parts of the ground
have fallen away. (Wessex)

Part of a continuous pattern of
cinquefoils within circles
powdered with lozenges, set in a
square with foliated motifs in the
spandrels and centre, alternating
with squares enclosing fleurs-de-
lys back to back. (Wessex, 35)

BIBLIOGRAPHY

BARNARD, J. (1972), 'Victorian Ceramic Tiles', Studio Vista, London.
EAMES, E.S. (1968), 'Mediaeval Tiles', British Museum Publications,
London.
'Records of Buckinghamshire', vol.XIV, Architectural & Archaeological
Society for the County of Buckingham, Aylesbury.
Catalogues from the Victoria & Albert Museum, London.

Clocks of various styles are to be found in Vestries and if the names of the styles are known much valuable time can be saved from the description.

The most usual are wall-hanging (the use of 'mural' should be avoided): clocks on shelves are known as shelf, mantel or bracket clocks: the one in the tower is known as a turret or tower clock. Other possible finds may be known as architectural, balloon, banjo, basket top, bell, beehive, carriage, Gothic (steeple or lancet), lantern, longcase, lyre, mirror, table and tavern - all of which will also be wall-hanging or mantel clocks except the longcase which is better known as 'grandfather' and table clocks on which the dial is on the top.

In most cases FURNITURE DESCRIPTIONS are applicable with the following additions:
The CASE contains the DIAL (face) and the MOVEMENT (works).
A longcase clock consists of a HOOD, TRUNK and BASE.
The BOB is the lenticular or pear-shaped weight at the end of the PENDULUM ROD.
The cylindrical lead, cast iron or brass-sheeted weights on the end of chains are known as WEIGHTS. In some primitive turret clocks the weights are of stone.
The LENTICLE is the correct name for the glass let into the door of a longcase clock to allow the motion of the bob to be seen, when glazed with thick green glass it is usually known as a 'bull's eye'. Lenticles became obsolete by 1710.
CALENDAR or DATE APERTURE - early 18th century clocks have one numeral in a square aperture, late 18th century ones may have three sets in a segmental aperture.
FRETS are pierced decorative brass pieces on lantern clocks, but wood or metal sound-reducing panels on other clocks.
HANDS are an indication of date until 1830, the mid 18th century hands being very delicate: country specimens continued to have only one hand until c.1780.
The LABEL giving details of clockmaker or cabinetmaker is important.
The TABLET, a rarely found decorative panel at the bottom is different from the SPLAT which is a decorative panel at the top of many clocks.
Roman NUMERALS (see LETTERING) were used for the hours, with Arabic minutes above them until after 1800.
SPANDREL and PILLAR decoration are an indication of date.

BIBLIOGRAPHY

BRUTON, E. (1967), 'Clocks and Watches, 1400-1900', Arthur Barker, London.
HUGHES, G.B. (1963), 'The Country Life Collector's Pocket Book', Hamlyn, London.
HUGHES, T. (1968), 'The Country Life Pocket Book of Furniture', Hamlyn, London.
McDONALD, J.W. (1965), 'Antique Furniture', Collins, London.
RAMSEY, L.G.G. (1962), 'The Complete Encyclopaedia of Antiques', The Connoisseur, London.

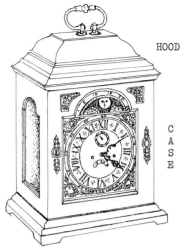

HOOD

C
A
S
E

Lunar dial

Spandrels
Seconds dial

Date aperture

Maker's name
Plinth and
Bracket feet

Fret

Lantern clock
with weights
c.1680

18th century mahogany Mantel,
Bracket or Shelf clock
Arched ornamental dial showing
phases of the moon, asymmetrical
rococo spandrels, key escutcheon
and matching blind escutcheon and
corner pieces flanking the lunar
dial. Wavy minute hand, Arabic
minute figures, plain silvered
chapter ring, seconds dial and
large date aperture.
Maker's name at base of applied
chapter ring (sample description).

Japanned Tavern,
Coaching Inn or
Act of Parliament
clock, c.1797

Weight-driven and
unglazed

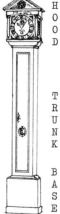

H
O
O
D

Gabled pediment
Fret

Glazed door (before
1690 the hood lifted off)

Square headed trunk door

T
R
U
N
K

Lenticle showing
pendulum rod and bob

B
A
S
E

Plinth

Late 17th century Architectural
Longcase clock with square dial

Hooded clock
with weights c.1745

Although biblical figures are often portrayed in mediaeval
or contemporary costume, authentic biblical dress was influenced by
that of the many lands with which the characters came in contact.
The basic Hebrew costume was the long tunic with girdle, loose open
cloak, sandals, nomad's headdress of square cloth bound with cord,
or pointed cap with or without a scarf wound around the base, and
the talith - a striped fringed prayer shawl. Women wore a long
tunic covered by a shawl or long veil.

The loose-fitting garment worn by Egyptians, Persians and
Byzantines is known as the Robe: an Egyptian woman's dress is a
kalasiris, sari or sheath, though sometimes she is shown wearing the
the robe only. The skirt worn by Egyptian men is known as a kilt or
loin cloth, sometimes with an apron, their blue and white striped
linen head covering with a cobra emblem attached to a gold fillet is
called a khat, the headgear resembling a hat is a crown. The Assyrian
pot-shaped hat is a mitre, a king sometimes wears a diadem headband.
An Israelite priest also wears a mitre or a turban with an inscribed
gold plate.

Crown

Kilt
Apron

Robe

Mitre

Arm-bands

Bracelets

Fringed and
Tasselled
Royal Cloak

Roman Officer
with Crested Helmet

Roman Legionary

Plain Helmet
with knob on
top

Military Cloak

Baldrick from
left shoulder

Cuirass with
pendant strips

Tunic

Shield
with
Thunder-
bolt
device

Laced Boots

Leggings

(Greek warriors
wore greaves and
carried circular
shields)

Sandals

Wreath (laurel)

Roman Patrician in
Tunic and Toga
(borders coloured
according to rank)

Plebeians wore a
Tunic and Cloak

A married Roman
lady wore a Palla
(not a Toga)
over her
Stola or
Dalmatic.

Greek men wore a
long or short Chiton
(tunic) and a large
Himation or a small
Chlamys over it.
Scholars sometimes
omitted the Chiton
giving the impression
of wearing a Toga.

Greek women
wore the
same as the
men, unless
they were
Amazons.

Phrygian Cap

Long or short
Veil

Super Tunic
pulled up into
belt

Knee-length
Tunic with
tight-fitting
sleeves

Braes with
crossbinding

Long cloak
(sometimes a
circular cloak
with head opening
near one edge)

Tunic

Short Braes

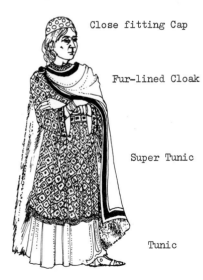

Close fitting Cap

Fur-lined Cloak

Super Tunic

Tunic

Fillet or Coronet
over Veil
and Wimple

Figure-fitting
Bliaut
with lined hanging
sleeves and
Corselet

Girdle wound
twice round
body

Mantle (cloak)
lined with fur
or contrasting
colour

Cap over
Coif

Cyclas
(sleeveless
surcoat)

Braes

Hose

Hood

Cotehardie
or Surcoat
worn over
an under-
tunic

Capuchon
over a
Wimple

Pelisse

Cotte

Fillet

Cloak with
dagged edges

Gipon with low belt
and buttoned sleeves

Hose

Crespine Headdress
consisting of
Fillet, Fret and
Barbette

Loose Surcoat
worn over

Cotte or
Kirtle

Widow's Veil

Wimple

Sideless
Cotehardie
worn over
a Kirtle

A widow known
as 'an Avowess'

Coif

Hood with
Liripipe

Hat worn over Hood

Chaplet

Wimple and Veil
13th century

Crespine
13th-14th century

Nebule
14th century

Gorget 14th century

Horned 15th century

French Hood
15th century

Reticulated
15th century

Butterfly
15th century

French Hood with
Bongrâce 15th century

Kennel or Gabled or
Pedimented
16th century

Hennin 15th century

Marie Stuart Cap
16th century

Prayer Beads
Purse
Annelace

Chaperon

Neckchain

Long Gown worn over
Doublet and Hose

Padded roll with veil attached
above a Fret

Houpelande (a voluminous
circular gown with hole in
centre for head and sliced at
sides to form pointed hanging
sleeves. High waisted for
women, normally placed waist
for men)

Kirtle

Jerkin
with slit
hanging
sleeves
worn
over
Doublet and
Hose
Belt with
tongue

Doublet

Hose

Pedimental Headdress

Veil

Linen Partlet
Low-necked Gown

Heraldic Mantle fastened by cords

Large Belt with Buckle and
attached ornaments on long ends
(the one illustrated has a
symbolic 3-rose buckle)

Flat Cap

Shirt

Doublet

Jerkin

Fur-lined Gown
worn as cloak

Trunk Hose
slashed and
padded at top

Square-toed shoes

French Hood

Ruff

Puffed
Sleeves

Gown with
Farthingale

Quilted
Petticoat
or
Kirtle

Wig

Cravat

Falling Band

Slashed Sleeves

Padded Doublet

Coif

Tassets
on Basque

Full Breeches

Collar

Tippet

Tall Hat with
Ribbons

Lace Collar

Doublet

Short
Doublet

Cloak

Knee
Breeches

Breeches

Pannier

Bucket-top
Boots

Gown with panniers

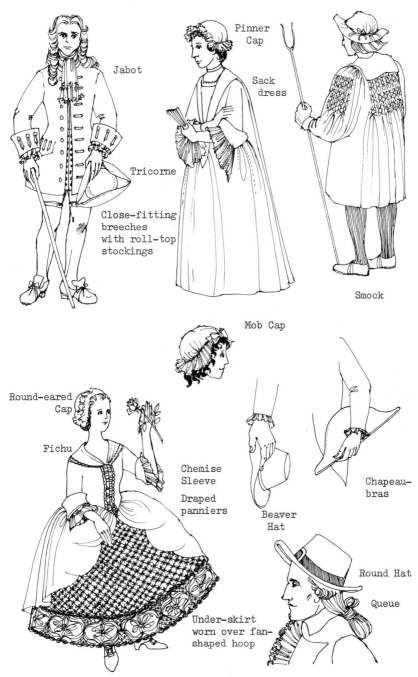

Jabot

Pinner Cap

Sack dress

Tricorne

Close-fitting breeches with roll-top stockings

Smock

Mob Cap

Round-eared Cap

Fichu

Chemise Sleeve

Draped panniers

Beaver Hat

Chapeau-bras

Round Hat

Queue

Under-skirt worn over fan-shaped hoop

Redingote, with full
skirts, rolled collar
and shoulder cape
Peg-top trousers

Sloping-away coat,
white facings,
waistcoat,
knee-breeches and
stockings,
epaulettes

Double-breasted
Cut-away coat
Bell-bottomed
trousers

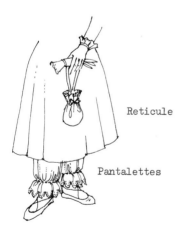

Reticule

Pantalettes

Frock coat

Morion Helmet

Cap

Sleeveless Jerkin

Doublet

Sash worn over
Cuirass

Swordbelt

Breeches

Hose

Thighboots

Tippet
(an academical
hood might be
added to or
substituted for
the tippet)

Gown, split in
front showing
Surplice worn
over Cassock

Soldier c.1590
with arquebus

Doctor c.1480

Red Cap
White undercap
Long beard and hair

White Cloak
with Red Cross
on shoulder
Staff with
metal shield
showing a
Red Cross
on a
White ground

Flat Helm

White
Surcoat with
Red Cross
on breast

Banded Mail

Knight Templar 13th century

Crusader 13th century

BIBLIOGRAPHY

DAVENPORT, MILLIA (1948), 'The Book of Costume', Crown Publishers, New York.
LISTER, M. (1967), 'Costume, An Illustrated Survey from Ancient Times to the 20th Century', Barrie & Jenkins, London.
'Encyclopaedia Britannica':   see Costume, Robes, Universities, Vestments.

Antelope, Hind, Hart,
Doe or Stag

Basilisk or
Cockatrice

Centaur

Dragon

Griffin

Dolphin

Phoenix

Salamander

Unicorn

Wodehose

Wyvern

Green Man

BIBLIOGRAPHY

CHILD, H. and COLLES, D. (1971), 'Christian Symbols Ancient and
Modern', Bell, London.
ELLWOOD POST, W. (1964), 'Saints, Signs and Symbols', SPCK, London.
GRIGSON, G. (1966), 'The Shell Country Alphabet' and 'The Shell
Country Book', Rainbird, London.

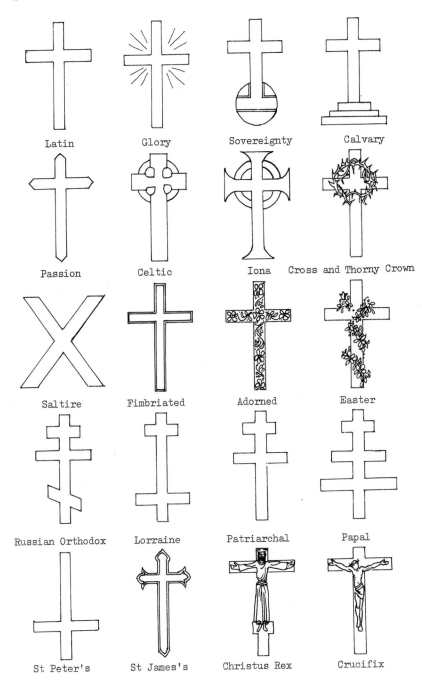

Latin   Glory   Sovereignty   Calvary

Passion   Celtic   Iona   Cross and Thorny Crown

Saltire   Fimbriated   Adorned   Easter

Russian Orthodox   Lorraine   Patriarchal   Papal

St Peter's   St James's   Christus Rex   Crucifix

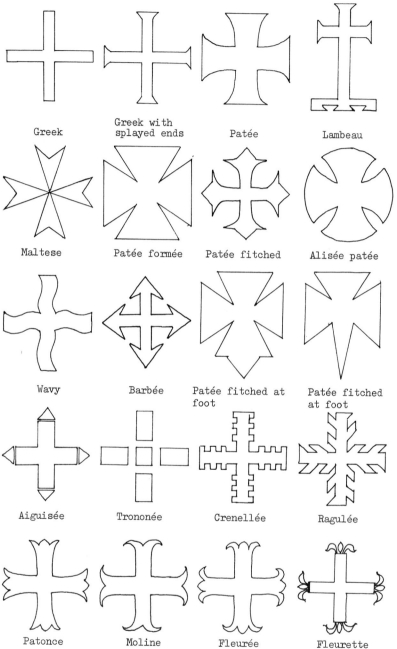

Greek

Greek with
splayed ends

Patée

Lambeau

Maltese

Patée formée

Patée fitched

Alisée patée

Wavy

Barbée

Patée fitched at
foot

Patée fitched
at foot

Aiguisée

Trononée

Crenellée

Ragulée

Patonce

Moline

Fleurée

Fleurette

Pommée

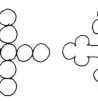

Bezant

Bottonée

Canterbury

Paternoster

Milrine

Clercée or
Entrailed

Cercelée

Four Pheons

Four Ermine
Spots

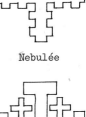

Nebulée

St Julian's

Cross Crosslet

Cross Crosslet
fitched

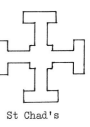

Crusader's or
Jerusalem

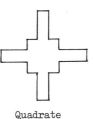

Cantonée

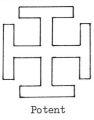

Degraded

Potent

St Chad's

Quadrate

Parted and Frettée   Triparted   Frettée   Masclée

Fylfot or   Potent Rebated   Chain   Looped
Swastika

Anchor   Anchor   Anchor   Anchor

Latin cross   Tau   Ankh   Crux Ansata
fleurée

Floriated   Circle and   Greek cross   Floriated
Quatrefoil   Quatrefoil   Fleurée   Octafoil

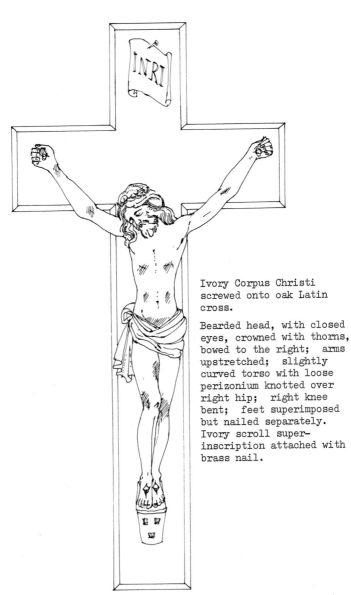

Ivory Corpus Christi screwed onto oak Latin cross.

Bearded head, with closed eyes, crowned with thorns, bowed to the right; arms upstretched; slightly curved torso with loose perizonium knotted over right hip; right knee bent; feet superimposed but nailed separately. Ivory scroll super-inscription attached with brass nail.

A CRUCIFIX is a cross with the image of Christ affixed.

When Christ is depicted wearing Eucharistic Vestments and a crown, it is known as a Crucifix of Christus Rex.

A figure with open eyes is 'Christ in Agony', with closed eyes it is 'the Dead Christ' or 'Corpus Christi'.

ACANTHUS

ANTHEMIUM or HONEYSUCKLE

BALL FLOWER

BAY LEAF

BEAD

BEAD AND REEL

BEED AND REEL

BEAKHEAD

BIFURCATED

BILLET (round)

BILLET (square)

BRATTISHING

CABLE

CHEVRON

DENTIL (straight or diagonal)

DIAPER (diamond reticulation)

DOG TOOTH

DOUBLE CONE

EGG AND TONGUE (or ovolo)

EGG AND DART

EMBATTLED, BATTLEMENTED,
CASTELLATED or CRENELLATED

FESTOON

FLEUR-DE-LYS

FOUR LEAF FLOWER

FRET or LATTICE or KEY
and sometimes MEANDER

GADROONING, LOBING or NULLING

GOUGING, CHANELLING or ADZED
usually called SCOOP

GUILLOCHE

HUSK

IMBRICATED interrupted by
Tudor ornament

INTERLACING (resembling
Strapwork and Moresque)

LOTUS alternating with PALMETTE

LOZENGE

LUNETTE

MEANDER

MORESQUE (16th century term for
interlacing)

NAILHEAD

OVOLO (convex moulding)

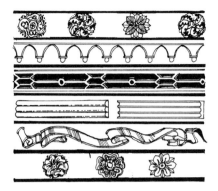

PATERA

PEARDROP

PIERCED

REEDING and FLUTING

RIBBON (sometimes 'ribband')

ROSETTE (rose-patterned patera)

SCALLOPED

SCRATCHWORK and CHIPCARVING
(a technique)

SCROLL (many variations)

SHELL

STRAPWORK

SWAG

TRACERY and
BLIND or APPLIED TRACERY

TRELLIS or LATTICE

TUDOR ORNAMENT

TUDOR ROSE

VINE

VITRUVIAN SCROLL or RUNNING DOG

WATERLEAF

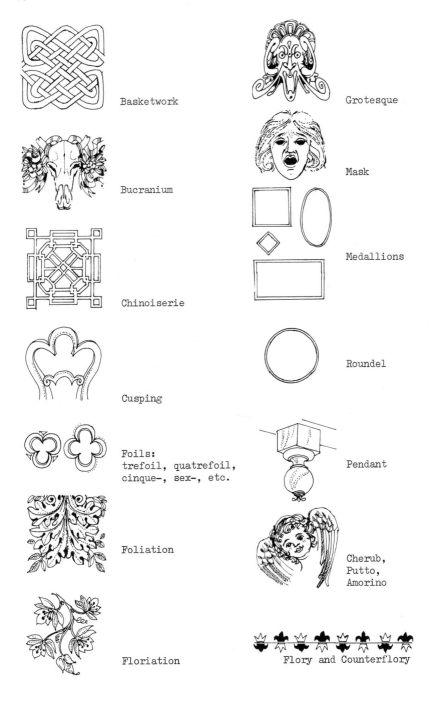

Basketwork

Bucranium

Chinoiserie

Cusping

Foils:
trefoil, quatrefoil,
cinque-, sex-, etc.

Foliation

Floriation

Grotesque

Mask

Medallions

Roundel

Pendant

Cherub,
Putto,
Amorino

Flory and Counterflory

VERTEBRATE band:
a continuous design, usually
of flowers, fruit or foliage,
with the main stem running
through the centre.

RUSTICATION:
any object or
material that
appears artificially
weathered.

UNDULATE band:
the main stem has a wavy
motion.

TROPHY:

a purely decorative group
of weapons, musical instruments,
armour or other memento, usually
displayed with foliations,
ribbons and flowers.

BIBLIOGRAPHY

BRACKETT, O. (n.d.), 'English Furniture Illustrated', Hamlyn,
London.
GLOAG, J. (1952), 'A Short Dictionary of Furniture', Allen & Unwin,
London.
MEYER, F.S. (1957), 'Handbook of Ornament', Dover, New York.
WARE, D. and STAFFORD, M. (1974), 'An Illustrated Dictionary of
Ornament', Allen & Unwin, London.

TREE OF JESSE

A standard subject of the mediaeval artist in carvings, manuscripts,
glass, paintings, etc., combining the prophecy of Isaiah with the
genealogical descent of Christ from David and his father Jesse as
given in St Matthew's Gospel, Chapter I. The figures on the
branches represent prophets, often in contemporary dress, who
proclaimed the coming of the Messiah, and the kings of Judah of
the line of David. The Virgin appears near the apex, holding the
Child or alone with the figure of Christ above her and the
descending Dove of the Holy Spirit, or doves representing the Gifts
of the Holy Spirit.

The TREE OF LIFE is depicted in innumerable ways, usually
naturalistic in form - it was widespread in art throughout the East
as a symbol of life and knowledge, long before the time of Christ.
To Christians it is the symbol of Salvation.

For the symbolism of all fruits, flowers and trees, readers are
referred to Heather Child and Dorothy Colles, 'Christian Symbols
Ancient and Modern', Bell, London, 1971.

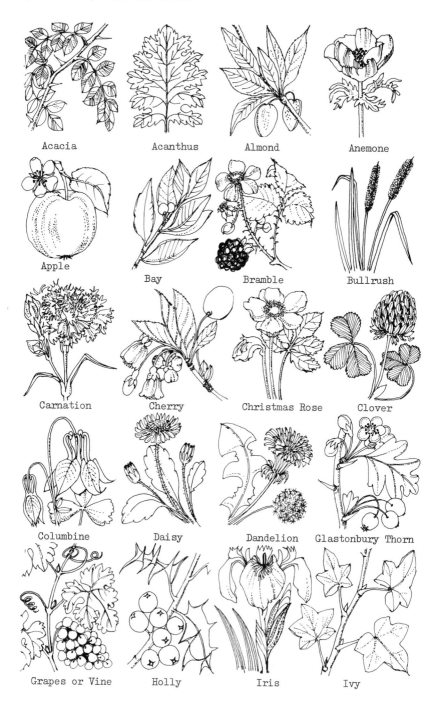

Acacia   Acanthus   Almond   Anemone

Apple
          Bay   Bramble   Bullrush

Carnation   Cherry   Christmas Rose   Clover

Columbine   Daisy   Dandelion   Glastonbury Thorn

Grapes or Vine   Holly   Iris   Ivy

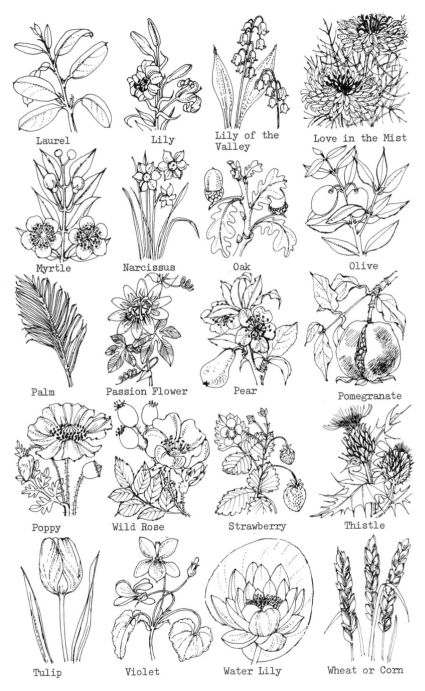

Laurel

Lily

Lily of the Valley

Love in the Mist

Myrtle

Narcissus

Oak

Olive

Palm

Passion Flower

Pear

Pomegranate

Poppy

Wild Rose

Strawberry

Thistle

Tulip

Violet

Water Lily

Wheat or Corn

The term FRAMEWORK is inclusive and applies to all sections. Every edging, rim, border, etc., enclosing something, is a frame, and in some cases the frame is a feature in itself. The term is also used for the skeleton or substructure of a piece of furniture.

There are two classes of architectural frames (used for doors, windows, panels, tablets, medallions, niches, soffits, pictures, books, etc.):
MON-AXIAL, those with external ornament top and bottom to emphasise the vertical, the lower ornament having the general shape of a bracket, and the upper making a cresting feature; and
BI-AXIAL, when the space enclosed is surrounded by ornament symmetrical on all sides.

When the frame resembles a scroll of parchment, with turned-up ends, it is termed a CARTOUCHE.

When the frame is cut into interlacing bands, it is termed a STRAPWORK FRAME and is characteristic of the Renaissance style. It appears on sepulchral monuments, on medals and coins, furniture, in heraldry, books, jewellery, on clocks, signs, escutcheons, etc., foliage and festoons being frequently added.

In books and documents, strapwork often includes lightly treated architectural forms.

BIBLIOGRAPHY

MEYER, F.S. (1957), 'Handbook of Ornament', Dover, New York.

An ACHIEVEMENT is the term for the complete armorial device, which includes shield, helm, crest, mantling, wreath, supporters, motto, etc., though some of these may not be included.

On plate an achievement or coat-of-arms are usually referred to as ARMORIALS.

A COAT-OF-ARMS is only what is displayed on the shield, lozenge or banner.

A CREST is the device borne on the helm of a noble or knight as a distinguishing mark.

A BADGE is not a crest - it is a device denoting membership of a community, or a strictly personal addition to a coat-of-arms.

Whilst the banner and shield of a noble or knight would display his arms, and his helmet bear his crest, his BADGE would be worn by his soldiers and servants. Some families had several badges and it is interesting to be able to recognise them. Women adopted badges but not crests, and women should not display a shield.

The personal arms of bishops are impaled by those of their Sees: the same principle applies to certain other officials.

The INSIGNIA is the term usually used for a display of the distinguishing marks of office or honour.

DEXTER is the left side of the person looking at the shield.
SINISTER is the right-hand side of the person looking at the shield.

A record of an achievement or coat-of-arms can be made, either by describing it in heraldic terms (blazoning), which requires a basic knowledge of the terms, or by tricking, the term used for making a rough sketch and giving EVERY DETAIL including all the colours and all the parts of animals, down to the last detail, so that someone else will be able to blazon it (see p.67).

In cases where it might be difficult to date, the shape of the shield should be included. It will be noticed that in general armouries the helmet and wreath are seldom described as they are understood to form part of the composition, but when tricking, it is advisable to include everything.

To identify a coat-of-arms, check whether there is a similar coat elsewhere in the church or graveyard, under which there may be a helpful inscription. The church leaflet, the incumbent, the local antiquary and members of the local reference library are useful sources of information. County histories often contain details of arms.

If the tricking is adequate, the arms should be traceable in either Burke's 'General Armoury' or Papworth's 'Ordinary of Armorials' (which is Burke in reverse) - with a little effort amateurs can easily find their way about both. It will not be possible to find every coat-of-arms and impossible to trace those assumed illegally during Victorian times!

Crest

*Mural Crown

Mantling

Helm

Supporters

Shield

Compartment

Motto

BADGE

Crest

**Wreath

Helm (according to his rank)
Mantling (drapery hanging from helm, not to
be confused with a mantle)

Shield (bearing the Coat-of-Arms)

**The wreath supports the
crest on the helm and is
composed of six twists,
curved or straight, in the
same tinctures as on the
shield, with metal always
the first on dexter.

Gauntlets

Spurs

Sword
(usually Regimental)

CHAPEAU

*Alternative to a wreath
or crest coronet, which
is not the same as a
coronet of rank.

INSIGNIA as usually displayed in churches

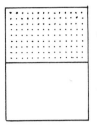

or (gold)

argent (silver) arg.

Any charge in
Natural Colours
is blazoned as
'proper' - ppr.

proper - ppr.

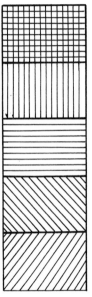

sable (black) sa.

gules (red) gu.

azure (blue) az.

Except for the arms of
Jerusalem

NO metal is ever placed
on metal,
NOR colour on colour,
NOR fur on fur

vert (green) vt.

purpure (purple) purp.

FURS

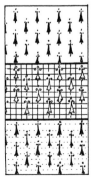

ermine
(arg. ermined sa.)

ermines
(sa. ermined arg.)

erminois
(or ermined sa.)

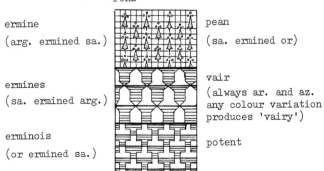

pean
(sa. ermined or)

vair
(always ar. and az.
any colour variation
produces 'vairy')

potent

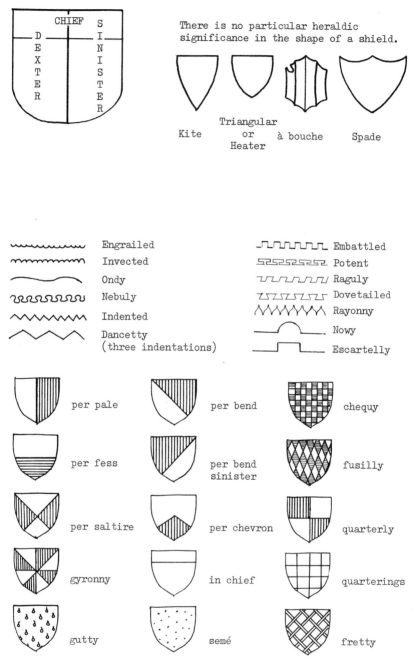

There is no particular heraldic
significance in the shape of a shield.

Kite

Triangular
or   à bouche   Spade
Heater

Engrailed

Invected

Ondy

Nebuly

Indented

Dancetty
(three indentations)

Embattled

Potent

Raguly

Dovetailed

Rayonny

Nowy

Escartelly

per pale

per fess

per saltire

gyronny

gutty

per bend

per bend
sinister

per chevron

in chief

semé

chequy

fusilly

quarterly

quarterings

fretty

CADENCY MARKS denote seniority in a family and sometimes distinguish one branch from another (used only in England).

| Eldest son | second | third | fourth | fifth | sixth |

| seventh | eighth | ninth |

Escutcheon of Pretence

indicates marriage to an heiress; her descendants are entitled to bear her arms - those on the escutcheon - as a quartering.

The Red Hand of Ulster

a distinguishing mark for Baronets other than baronets of Nova Scotia.

The numbering of a simple quartered shield.

A shield with more quarterings is beyond the scope of these notes, although it is suggested that the number of quarters be given and the blazon or tricking of the first quarter.

Per pale or and gu. three roundels counterchanged. (sample description or blazon)

DUKE'S Coronet

8 strawberry leaves
of equal height; only
5 appearing in illustrations
and when used as a charge
or a crest only 5 showing.

MARQUESS'S Coronet

4 strawberry leaves
alternating with
4 pearls of equal height.

In illustrations, 3 leaves
and 2 pearls are shown.

EARL'S Coronet

8 pearls on long points
alternating with
8 short strawberry leaves.

In illustrations, 5 pearls
and 4 leaves are shown.

VISCOUNT'S Coronet

16 pearls on the rim.

In illustrations only
8 or 9 pearls are shown.

BARON'S Coronet

6 pearls on the rim.

In illustrations only
4 pearls are shown.

A KING
and his Sons
and Brothers

4 crosses patée
alternating with
fleurs-de-lys

On the King's
Crown, diadems
spring from the
crosses and the
junction is
surmounted by a
mount bearing
another cross
patée.

His eldest son's
Coronet is
similar but with
only two diadems.

Coronets of the
younger sons, and
brothers, of kings
are destitute of
arch and orb and
are surmounted by
a golden tassel.

ROYAL HELMET

gold,
six bars,
affrontée

DUKE AND MARQUESS

gold and steel,
five bars,
affrontée

EARL, VISCOUNT AND BARON

silver, garnished with gold,
four or five bars,
shown in profile

BARONET OR KNIGHT

steel,
vizor raised,
affrontée

GENTLEMAN OR ESQUIRE

steel,
vizor closed,
shown in profile

A HATCHMENT shows the armorial bearings of a deceased person.
Not to be confused with an ARMORIAL PANEL, it is usually painted on
canvas stretched across a lozenge-shaped frame, heavily painted to
withstand the weather, the silver and gold indicated by white and
yellow. The heraldry is seldom accurate and the motto not always
that of the family.

There are well defined rules as to the arrangement of the arms
according to the marital state, sex and rank of the deceased.

The DEXTER side is the male side (except for Bishops).

Variations occur when the arms of more than one wife are depicted
on a hatchment.

Most important is the background surrounding the arms - it is
ALWAYS BLACK around those of the deceased.

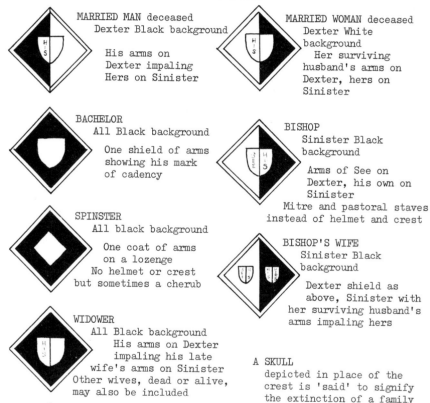

MARRIED MAN deceased
Dexter Black background

His arms on
Dexter impaling
Hers on Sinister

MARRIED WOMAN deceased
Dexter White
background
Her surviving
husband's arms on
Dexter, hers on
Sinister

BACHELOR
All Black background

One shield of arms
showing his mark
of cadency

BISHOP
Sinister Black
background

Arms of See on
Dexter, his own on
Sinister
Mitre and pastoral staves
instead of helmet and crest

SPINSTER
All black background

One coat of arms
on a lozenge
No helmet or crest
but sometimes a cherub

BISHOP'S WIFE
Sinister Black
background

Dexter shield as
above, Sinister with
her surviving husband's
arms impaling hers

WIDOWER
All Black background
His arms on Dexter
impaling his late
wife's arms on Sinister
Other wives, dead or alive,
may also be included

A SKULL
depicted in place of the
crest is 'said' to signify
the extinction of a family

WIDOW
All Black background

Arms on a lozenge, her late husband's on Dexter
impaling hers on Sinister
Crest, helm and motto omitted, a knot of ribbon
perhaps taking their place

A TRICKING

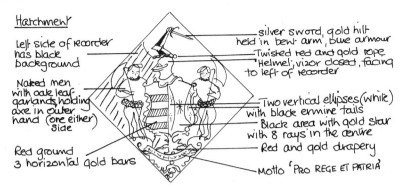

Hatchment

Left side of recorder has black background

Naked men with oak leaf garlands, holding axe in outer hand (one either side)

Red ground 3 horizontal gold bars

silver sword, gold hilt held in bent arm, blue armour

Twisted red and gold rope

Helmet, vizor closed, facing to left of recorder

Two vertical ellipses (white) with black ermine tails

Black area with gold star with 8 rays in the centre

Red and gold drapery

Motto 'PRO REGE ET PATRIA'

N.B. The BLAZON given under has been checked with Burke's 'General Armory' and 'Peerage', but in the HATCHMENT the savages do not appear to be wreathed about the head.

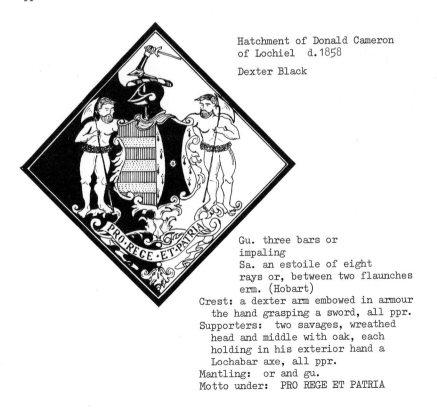

Hatchment of Donald Cameron of Lochiel d. 1858

Dexter Black

Gu. three bars or
impaling
Sa. an estoile of eight
rays or, between two flaunches
erm. (Hobart)

Crest: a dexter arm embowed in armour
  the hand grasping a sword, all ppr.
Supporters: two savages, wreathed
  head and middle with oak, each
  holding in his exterior hand a
  Lochabar axe, all ppr.
Mantling: or and gu.
Motto under: PRO REGE ET PATRIA

Pre-1340

Gules, three lions passant gardant in pale or.

1340-1405

1 and 4   France
2 and 3   England

N.B. Old France, semé de fleurs-de-lys (semé-de-lis).

1405-1603

1 and 4   France
2 and 3   England

N.B. Only three fleurs-de-lys.

1603-1707

1 and 4 Quarterly France and England
2 Scotland (or, a lion ramp. within a double
            tressure flory counterflory gu.)
3 Ireland (az. a harp or, stringed arg.)

1689-1702

1 and 4 Quarterly France and England
2   Scotland
3   Ireland

An escutcheon az. charged with a lion ramp. or was added between 1689-1702.

1707-1801

1 and 4 England impaling Scotland (see below)
2 France
3 Ireland

N.B. From 1714 the White Horse of Hanover was added, either in the centre or in the 4th quarter.

1801-1837

1 and 4 England
2 Scotland
3 Ireland
The arms of Hanover in centre.

1837 -

ARMS Quarterly, 1st and 4th, gu. three lions pass. gard. in pale or
for ENGLAND: 2nd, or, a lion ramp. within a double tressure flory
counterflory gu., for SCOTLAND: 3rd, az, a harp or, stringed ar.,
for IRELAND: the whole encircled with the Garter.

CREST Upon the royal helmet the imperial crown ppr., thereon statant
gardant or, a lion imperially crowned also ppr.

SUPPORTERS Dexter, a lion ramp. gard., or, crowned as the crest;
sinister, an unicorn arg. armed, crined and unguled or, gorged with
a coronet composed of crosses pattée and fleurs-de-lys, a chain
affixed thereto, passing between the fore-legs, and reflexed over
the back, of the last.

MOTTO DIEU ET MON DROIT, in the compartment below the shield; with
the Union rose, shamrock and thistle engrafted on the same stem.

CROWN of ENGLAND A circle of gold, issuing therefrom four crosses
pattée and four fleurs-de-lys, arranged alternately: from the
crosses pattée arise two arched and golden diadems, ornamented with
pearls, closing at the top under a mound, surmounted by a cross
pattée, also gold, the whole enriched with precious stones: cap of
crimson velvet, turned up erm.

BADGES ENGLAND The red and white rose united
        SCOTLAND A thistle
        IRELAND A harp or, the strings arg.
        IRELAND A shamrock leaf vert.
        WALES A dragon pass. wings elevated gu. upon a
               mound vert.
All ensigned with the royal crown.

Illustrations of THE BRITISH ORDERS OF KNIGHTHOOD will be found in
Burke's and other books of reference: most are recognisable by the
devices on the Insignia and the motto:

The Garter (buckle) 'Honi soit qui mal y pense'.

The Thistle (saltire cross and thistle) 'Nemo me impune lacessit'.

St Patrick (shamrock) 'Quis separabit'.

The Bath (Maltese Cross with rose, thistle and shamrock in centre)
'Tria Juncta in Uno'.

Star of India 'Heaven's Light our Guide'.

St Michael and St George 'Auspicium Melioris Aevi'.

Victoria and Albert (in profile).

Savages and Saracens are a white race and bearded.
Saracens are clothed and wreathed about the temple.
Savages are naked and wreathed about the temple and loins.
Blackamoors are negroid, often with a serpent around the neck.

Some LIONS (other creatures have other postures)

rampant   rampant gardant   rampant regardant   salient

statant   passant   sejant   couchant

dormant   two lioncels   lioncels   lion rampant
              addorsed   combatant   double-headed

Much of the above notes has been condensed from a booklet which all members of NADFAS would enjoy:

PETER C. SUMMERS, FSA (1967), 'How to read a Coat of Arms', illustrated by Anthony Griffiths, B.Arch., published for The Standing Conference for Local History by RPS Ltd, Victoria Hall, Fingal St, London, SE10 0RF. 50p.

Published by Phillimore & Co. and by the same author, are county volumes entitled 'Hatchments in Britain', with some volumes still to appear.

As an introduction, 'Simple Heraldry, Cheerfully Illustrated' by IAIN MONCREIFFE and DON POTTINGER (1952), published by Nelson, is recommended.

BURKE, SIR BERNARD (1884), 'The General Armory of England, Scotland, Ireland and Wales', Burke's Peerage Ltd, London.
FOX-DAVIES, A.C. (1902), 'Armorial Families', T.C. & E.C. Jack, London.
FOX-DAVIES, A.C. (1909), 'Complete Guide to Heraldry', Nelson, London.
FRANLYN, J. (1965), 'Heraldry', Arco Publications, London (really useful for beginners).
MILBOURNE, J.S. (1950), 'Heraldry', W. & G. Foyle Ltd, London (a handbook).
PAPWORTH, J.W. (1874), 'Ordinary of British Armorials', Tabard Press, London.

The arms of the SEES, and of Canterbury and York, the two PROVINCES of the Church of England, will be found in 'Crockfords Clerical Directory'.

CANTERBURY

Az. an archiepiscopal
cross in pale or
surmounted by a pall ppr.
charged with four crosses
patée fitchée sa.

YORK

Gu. two keys
in saltire arg.
in chief a
regal crown.

ROMAN

MAJUSCULES (maj.) AS FOVND ON THE MONVMENT TO TRAIAN AD 114
the letters J,K,U,W,Y,Z were added later.

Roman minuscules or (min.) **small romans**

SQVARE Roman 2-6th centuries

RVSTIC Roman 3-6th centuries

UNCJAL Roman 4-8th centuries

Roman lettering returned to England late in the 15th century but was not in general use until c.1590.

LOMBARDIC UNCIALS
half unciuls
7-13th centuries

GOTHIC or Black letter
13-15th centuries

Under thys Tombe lyeth buryed the Wyfe of S˟ Edmond Bray knyght daughter of S˟ John Bowyer.

Italic, based on an oval and slightly sloping The angle of inclination distinguishes Roman from Italic.

Script often erroneously described as is based on contemporary cursive writing. *Copperplate*

'Gothick' and 'Lombardick' is the spelling often used to describe mid 18th century lettering. For later copies of the styles it is advisable to use the term 19th century Gothic or 20th century Lombardic.

CONTRACTIONS are freely used and should not be ignored.

Jesu   Christi   Filium   Propheta   And

COPPERPLATE   refers to the copper plate, not the cursive script.

CURSIVE   running or joined minuscules, the opposite of uncial
              or print.

CYPHER   an alternative to MONOGRAM - linked, interlaced,
              repeated or reversed letters - usually initials.

FILIGREE   decoration of simple forms and symbols.

ILLUMINATED   much decorated.

INITIAL LETTER   first letter of any word.

KNOT   basketwork ornament, sometimes used as a starting
              point for a filigree border where an initial letter
              is lacking: related to the weaving of a hollow
              letter.

LOGO   20th century term for sign or character representing a
              word as in shorthand.

MAJUSCULES and MINUSCULES (maj. and min.) Capitals and small letters.

RUBRICATION   addition of red, or other coloured letters,
              line-finishings or signs, to a black text.

SERIFS and TERMINALS   thin hairstrokes added to letters.

              SWASH, DOTS and FLOURISHES capitals less ornamented
              than when illuminated but often having
              intricate interwoven scrolling.

UNCIALS   majuscules of 4-8th centuries resembling 20th century
              capitals.

  HALF UNCIALS mixed maj. and min. of 7-9th centuries.

UPPER CASE and LOWER CASE (u/c and l/c) printers' terms for
                                          capitals and small letters.

VERSALS   coloured majuscules used to mark the beginnings of
              verses and paragraphs. Early versals are usually
              Roman, the later more ornate versals may be Lombardic.

ΕΟΙΣ ΕΠΙ ΑΡΙΣΤΑΓΟΡΑ
ΑΡΧΩΝΤΟΣ ΕΝΔΕΛΦΟΙΣ

Δέδυκε μὲν ἀ σελάννα
Κὰι Πληιάδες μέσαι δὲ
Νύκτες, παρὰ δ' ἔρχει' ὥρα
Ἔγω δὲ μόνα κατεύδω

GREEK

A CHRONOGRAM
is a phrase, etc., of which
the Roman-numeral letters
added give a date:

LorD haVe MerCIe Vpon Vs
=50+500+5+1000+100+1+5+5
= 1666

NUMERALS			NUMERALS	
ROMAN	ARABIC		ROMAN	ARABIC
I	1		MCCXXXIV	1234
II	2		MCCCCXCII	1492
III	3		MDIX	1509
IV	4		MDCCXXIX	1729
V	5		MDCCXLVII	1747
VI	6		MDCCCLXVIII	1868
VII	7		MDCCCXCIX	1899
VIII	8		MCMXVIII	1918
IX	9		MCMXLV	1945
X	10		MCMLXXVII	1977
XI	11			
XII	12			
XIII	13			
XIV	14			
XV	15			
XVI	16			
XVII	17			
XVIII	18			
XIX	19			
XX	20			
XXX	30			
XL	40			
L	50			
LX	60			
LXX	70			
LXXX	80			
XC	90			
C	100			
CCCC	400			
D or CCCCC	500			
M	1000			

Examples of LETTERING will be found among
the London Assay Marks:

Lombardic	1478-97, 1518-37, 1598-1617
Black Letter	1498-1517, 1558-77
	1658-77, 1678-97, 1756-75,
	1836-55, 1856-75, 1916-35
Court Hand	1638-57, 1697-1715
Italic	1618-37, 1956-
Roman	1538-57, 1578-97, 1716-35,
	1736-55, 1776-95, 1796-1815,
	1816-35, 1876-95, 1896-1915,
	1936-55

BIBLIOGRAPHY

JOHNSTON, E. (1906), 'Writing and Illuminating and Lettering',
Pitman, London.
MACKLIN, H.W. (1907), 'The Brasses of England', rev. 1975, E.P.
Group of Companies, Wakefield.

Memorials are usually tablets with an inscription in some sort of frame, and can be described in the manner of a piece of furniture or architecture by being broken-up into the parts around the tablet.

13th-15th century memorials are splendid examples of the mediaeval craftsman's work and were originally coloured or gilded, traces of which can sometimes be found. Heraldry, by which persons and marriages between families may be identified, should be recorded and note made of the way heraldic tints and metals may be recognised where there is no colour. Until the Restoration figures are usually representative.

For a complete description of a memorial Recorders should consult the sections on ARCHITECTURAL TERMS, BRASSES, ARMS AND ARMOUR, COSTUME, HERALDRY, LETTERING, SHAPES and VESTMENTS. As a guide the following details are important:

TYPE	free-standing, table or altar tomb, wall monument, wall tablet, floor slab, etc.
SUBJECT	
SCULPTOR	or attribution, if so give reference and state whether signed and if so, where.
DATE	with references (perhaps an account may be found).
LOCATION	
PHOTOGRAPHY	if photographs are available, state where.
DESCRIPTION	
INSCRIPTION	with texts in full, and give the type of lettering.
MATERIAL	stone, marble, alabaster, slate, terracotta, coadstone, plaster/stucco - or two or more materials.
SURFACE	painted, unpainted, gilded ....
CONDITION	parts missing, if so where they may be found. State if there is any record of alteration or move. Any damage.
DIMENSIONS	

Note should be made that bodies and memorials tend to get moved – a slab on a wall will not necessarily have a body under it, in spite of the wording of the inscription - it may previously have been a coffin-lid, or set in the floor - the same applies to BRASSES. Early memorials are barely decorated and mainly of interest for the lettering.

The use of the term 'Ledger' for a FLOOR SLAB should be avoided, as it is also used for 'registers'. 'WALL MEMORIAL' is preferable to 'mural'. The term 'mural' should be reserved for wall paintings.

Before 1275 slabs were smaller at the foot end.

In the 12th and 13th centuries local materials, including iron, were used. The earlier slabs, without lettering, were ornamented with a cross and circle, or carved or incised with symbols of the profession of the deceased. Later slabs might bear a carved representation of the deceased, though not always a true likeness - in both stone and brasses, the same figure may be found in different churches.

13th-17th century Brasses (thin pieces of metal, a mixture of copper and zinc) were let flush into the stones - see section on BRASSES. Slabs with INDENTS from which the brass is missing should be carefully described as they are of great interest.

The 17th and 18th centuries were the period when massive carved slabs of marble, or a bluish-grey stone (coadstone), were used, with often an achievement in bas-relief and the inscription incised in Roman lettering - reference to the language in the section on BRASSES will help.

 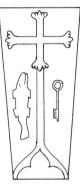 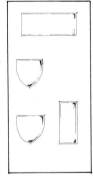 

| 12th or 13th century stone Coffin Cover with cross in relief | 13th century with incised cross and emblems | 14th century stone with indents (brasses missing) | 17th century grey marble with bas-relief achievement in roundel above the inscription |

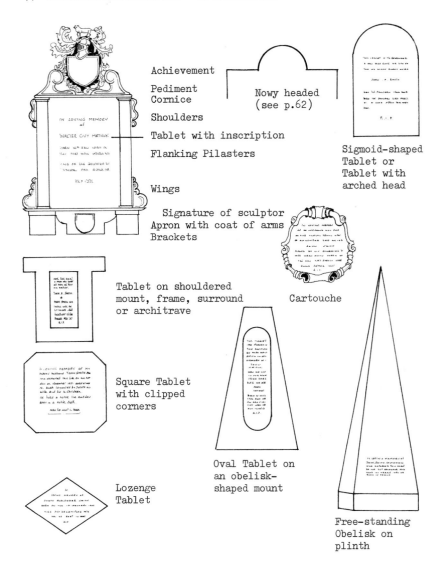

Achievement

Pediment
Cornice

Nowy headed
(see p.62)

Shoulders

Tablet with inscription

Flanking Pilasters

Wings

Sigmoid-shaped
Tablet or
Tablet with
arched head

Signature of sculptor
Apron with coat of arms
Brackets

Cartouche

Tablet on shouldered
mount, frame, surround
or architrave

Square Tablet
with clipped
corners

Oval Tablet on
an obelisk-
shaped mount

Lozenge
Tablet

Free-standing
Obelisk on
plinth

Bi-axial rectangular brass Tablet with
concave corners. Incised and black
inlaid cursive vine border. Similar
script inscription, with flourished
capitals, beginning and ending with a
rubricated patée cross. (sample
description)

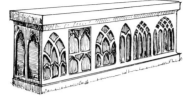

ALTAR or TABLE TOMB
with, or without, an
effigy lying on top.

Those against the North wall of
the Chancel are known as
EASTER SEPULCHRES.
They do not usually have a
figure, but may be canopied.

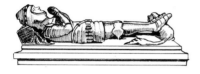

EFFIGIES
prior to the Reformation are
shown in a reverent attitude:
kneeling position popular in
16th century, more relaxed in
17th century. Actual portraits
unlikely until Restoration.

WEEPERS around tombs

Children carrying skulls
denotes their decease before
that of their parents.

BEDESMAN - pensioners of the deceased, bound to
          pray for his/her soul.

CADAVER

1550-EARLY 17th CENTURY
Renaissance ideas superseded Gothic forms, characterised by the
use of columns, obelisks, strapwork, grotesques and pavilions or
canopies. Poses are stiff, either recumbent or kneeling reverently.
Roman lettering mostly although Gothic still used in the provinces.
Contemporary dress. Painted and gilded alabaster very popular.
Notable sculptors: Maximilian Colt, Gerard and Nicholas Johnson,
William and Cornelius Cure.

MID 17th CENTURY
Classical style now more refined. In addition to the above poses,
some busts or head and shoulders framed in oval openings and
sometimes with architectural surrounds or pavilions. Contemporary
dress. White and black marble competing with alabaster.
Notable sculptors: Nicholas Stone, Edward and Joshua Marshall and
the Christmas family. Few signatures until late 17th century, and
even then, a mason who erected a monument and perhaps executed part
of the architectural background might sign the work.

c.1660 - EARLY 18th CENTURY
Baroque treatment of architectural surrounds: life-size figures in
contemporary costume: not much armour. Allegorical figures such as
Justice, Truth, Faith and Hope, and a tendency to represent patrons
in the heroic Roman manner but with contemporary details such as
wigs and square-toed shoes. Marble supersedes alabaster.
Notable sculptors: Grinling Gibbons, Arnold Quellin, John Nost,
Thomas Green, Caius Gabriel Cibber, Francis Bird, William and Edward
Stanton, William Kent, Edward Pierce, Christopher Cass, James Gibbs,
Giovanni Battista Guelfi, Peter Scheemakers and Laurent Delvaux.

MID 18th CENTURY
Figures dressed as Romans, sometimes in armour, sometimes in loosely
wrapped toga-like garments, standing or reclining on a sarcophagus
or against an urn, usually with a black marble pyramidal background.
Many small portrait medallions, putti, busts and cartouches.
Notable sculptors: Louis François Roubiliac, John Michael Rysbrack,
Henry, Peter and Thomas Scheemakers, Henry Cheere, Joseph Wilton.

LATE 18th AND EARLY 19th CENTURIES
More restrained classical style with enthusiasm for everything
Greek. Many mourning female figures draped over urns. Little
contemporary dress except for naval and military figures. Notable
sculptors: Joseph Nollekens, John Bacon and his son John, Richard
Westmacott, John Flaxman, Francis Chantrey, John Francis Moore.

VICTORIAN ERA
Still some mourning figures but also a revival of the Gothic style.
All styles of lettering.

BIBLIOGRAPHY

COLLINSON, H. (1975), 'Country Monuments, Their Families and
Houses', David & Charles, Newton Abbot.
ESDAILE, K. (1946), 'English Church Monuments', Batsford, London.
GUNNIS, R. (1953), 'Dictionary of British Sculptors 1660-1851',
Abbey Library, London.
PHYSICK, J. (1969), 'Designs for English Sculpture 1680-1860', HMSO,
London.

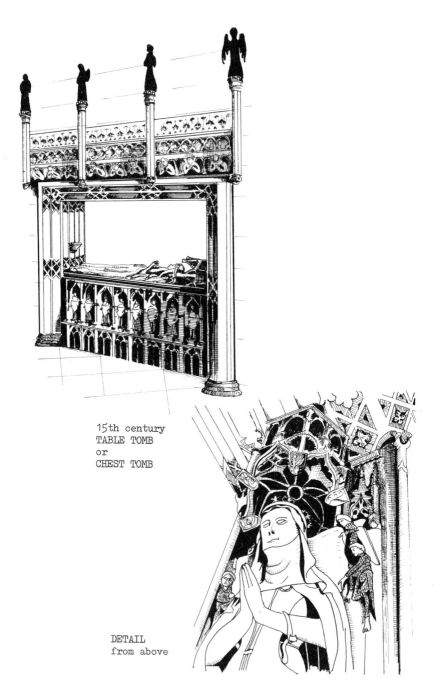

15th century
TABLE TOMB
or
CHEST TOMB

DETAIL
from above

The Table Tomb of Alice, Duchess of Suffolk, d.1475.
Made of alabaster, it was probably erected, soon after her
death, either in the chancel or in St John's Chapel - it
appears to have been shortened (ref. Church Guide, 1967).

The monument stands under a canopy of panelled stone, with
an elaborate cornice of tiers, the lowest formed of winged demi-
figures, each with hands folded on the breast; every alternate
head wears a crown, the others seem to have the tonsure and one
of them has a cross on his forehead. Above the figures is a
band of quatrefoils. The uppermost tier is formed of the
Tudor flower.

The canopy is divided vertically into three equal sections
by stone pillars with foliated bosses attached to the bases
and the capitals crested with battlementing on which stand carved
wooden figures, four on each side. (N.B. The figures should be
described.)

The actual tomb also consists of three tiers - on the top is
the recumbent figure of the Duchess clothed in the habit of a
vowess with a ducal coronet on her head, a ring on the third
finger of the right hand, and on the left fore-arm is the Garter.
Her hands are folded in prayer and her head rests on a cushion
supported by two angels on each side. Above her head is a most
elaborate canopy carved from a single block of alabaster. At
her feet is a lion. Above her feet, on the panelling, is a
bracket presumably for flowers or lights?

The sides of the tomb chest, on which the Duchess lies, is
carved with blind arcading in which are angels bearing shields
with coats-of-arms. (N.B. The angels and the shields should be
fully described and blazoned unless the arms are well known.)
Brass fillets on the cornice of the tomb chest, on both north and
south sides, carry the inscription in Black Lettered Latin.
The inscription reads ....

Below the chest is an open space, enclosed by an arcade of
eight arches on either side, within which may be seen a cadaver
clothed in a shroud. On the roof of this compartment, only to
be seen by lying on the floor and looking through the arcades,
are two frescoes, St Mary Magdalen and St John on one side and
the Annunciation on the other - a copy of which may be seen on
the Chancel side of the entrance to the Chapel.

The canopy, side-panelling and lowest tier of the tomb are
unpainted. The Duchess, and everything on her level, and the
tomb chest are parcel gilt and painted.

DIMENSIONS   ....

CONDITION   excellent.

LOCATION   Dividing the south side of the Chancel from
               St John's Chapel.

PHOTOGRAPHS   may be obtained in the Church, St Mary's, Ewelme.

WALL MEMORIAL   Nave N wall E

Rectangular mon-axial archi-
tecturally framed alabaster tablet
in memory of Richard Hampden
d. 1662 and his wife Ann d. 1663.

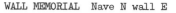

The cream alabaster tablet has
a plain black marble border.

The marble frame is flanked by
white-veined, free-standing,
angled Ionic columns which
support a moulded cornice and
segmental pediment with black
tympanum, against which and
protruding above is a painted
achievement.

Grey marble, acanthus
scrolled, tapering wing
brackets flank the tablet
against the wall.

The tablet and columns rest
on a black marble shelf
supported by black erect
consoles with white marble
architraves, between which,
set against the wall, is a
shield with a painted coat
of arms.

On tablet:

Here lyeth ye body of
RICHARD HAMPDEN
Cittizen of London
third son of
Sr EDMVND HAMPDEN
of ABBINGDON in ye COUNTY of
NORTHAMPTON. He departed
this life the nihth day of
September 1662

And also the body of
ANN
his wife the daughter of
FRANCIS LANE
Cittizen of London
She departed this life
the ninth day of
March 1663

Inscribed in incised Roman maj. and min.:

'Here lyeth ye body of/RICHARD HAMPDEN/Citizen of London/third
son of Sr EDMVND HAMPDEN/of ABBINGDON in ye COUNTY of/
NORTHAMPTON. He departed/this life the ninth day of/
September 1662./' gap 'And also the body of/ANN/his wife the
daughter of/FRANCIS LANE/Citizen of London./She departed this
life/the ninth day of/March 1663.'

Achievement on pediment:
    Ar. a saltire gu. betw. four eagles displ. az.
    A crescent for difference.
    Crest: A talbot statant erm. collared, ringed and lined gu. the
            end of the line tied in a knot over his back.
    Mantling: ar. and gu. (HAMPDEN)

Arms below memorial:
    Hampden impaling per pale az. and gu, three saltires couped ar.
                                                            (LANE)

N.B. The motto is not displayed on the memorial.

Sculptor's signature 'N.O.N.E.' on right edge of shelf.

Dimensions ... cm h. x ... cm w. Condition excellent - unpainted.

PHOTOGRAPH may be obtained from NADFAS ....

WALL MONUMENT in Chancel on N wall dedicated by Robert Hampden to the memory of his great-grandfather (The Patriot) and to his Benefactor John Hampden.   Attributed to Sir Henry Cheere and erected 1743 (ref. N. Pevsner). Approx. 2.40 m h. x 1.52 m w. - white and pink veined marble.

Sarcophagus with a putto sitting at either end of the lid, one holding a staff with a cap of liberty, the other a scroll inscribed 'Magna Charta'.   In the centre of the lid is an acanthus spray with ribbands stretching to the putti.

Directly above is an oval bas-relief with ribband cresting and moulded frame, depicting an oak tree hung with coloured shields of Hampdens and allied families, rising from a scene of Chalgrove Battle Field (where The Patriot John Hampden was slain in 1643).

On the front of the Sarcophagus is an inscription in Roman maj. and min., straight and slanting, relating to John Hampden d.1754 and showing his descent from The Patriot.

On the apron, between scrolled and acanthus decorated brackets and with an acanthus spray below the shaped bottom edge, is the dedication in the same lettering.

The Inscription reads ....
The Dedication reads ....

The Condition is excellent. Only the shields are painted.

The shields on the tree include the arms of Hampden, Symeon, Paget, Foley, Cornwallis, Waller, Hobart, Trevor, Van Kruningen and others not identified but blazoned by G. Lipscombe in his 'History of Buckinghamshire', 1822.

PHOTOGRAPH may be obtained from NADFAS ....

18th century WALL MONUMENT

Altar pedestal, bearing a large sarcophagus of grey marble, upon which reclines the statue of the earl in Roman tunic and toga, with the draped figure of Religion by his side, holding an open book in her left hand.

The front of the sarcophagus bears a medallion containing a bust of Sir William Petty, the earl's father and founder of the family.

On each side of the monument there are a pair of composite columns supporting a broken triangular pediment, upon the apex of which is a large vase filled with delicately sculpted foliage and flowers, and upon one side reclines the figure of Justice, and upon the other, that of Truth. Below the feet of each is an urn.

Immediately under the arch is an achievement, the arms being ermine, in a bend azure, a magnetic needle pointing to the Polar star.

A little below, against a tapering back panel swathed with drapery, are two cherubs among clouds holding a crown over the head of the expiring nobleman.

Standing upon the pedestal to the left of the sarcophagus is a male Roman in senatorial robes by the side of a statue of Charity who is seated and holds an infant at her breast. To the right are statues of Virtue and Wisdom guiding a child in front of them.

The monument is made entirely of marble, the sarcophagus, columns, arch, etc. of variously coloured stone and the twelve figures of white marble - all life size.

There is a long inscription in the centre of the pedestal in Roman lettering, reading

To the Memory
of Henry Petty, Earl of Shelburne,
Son of Sir William Petty

His Lordship married ....

The monument measuring approx. 8.19 m h. x 5.45 m w. (enclosed by an iron railing erected in 1755) is attributed to Scheemakers and cost £2,000.

(Ref. 'Records of Buckinghamshire', vol.VII, p.449.)

CONDITION requires cleaning.

PHOTOGRAPH in Church Guide (1976) by Herbert Green, published by The Church Publishers, Ramsgate, Kent.

N.B. The fragment leaning against the pedestal is part of the memorial to the earl's daughter - see ref. xyz.

The following illustrations consist mostly of the basic shapes, with an amalgamation of ornamental motifs relative to certain periods, which in many cases are derived from contemporary architecture, so that comparison with articles made of other materials is advantageous.

Further terms for the shapes of the various parts will be found in the section on SHAPES and further decorative terms in that on DECORATION. The HERALDRY and ARCHITECTURAL sections may also be required.

To save space, the following details have not been given in all the sample descriptions, but should always be recorded:

material, marks, measurements, inscriptions, details of armorials.

Engraved inscriptions and the costumes on figures are not a safe guide to the date of an article as the engravings may have been added at a later date and according to contemporary use of lettering, language and dress.

It will be noted that the name 'CHALICE' is used for Communion Cups until the Reformation (or approximately 1525), from which time 'COMMUNION CUP' is used and the designs appear more secular. 'CHALICE' is again used for the ornate designs towards the end of the 18th century during the Gothick Revival and also for the 19th and 20th century cups influenced by the Gothic and pre-Reformation Tudor designs. It should be noted that the latter tend to be larger than the originals and the jewels facetted and delicately mounted, whereas the earlier jewels were usually cabochon.

A few terms for metalwork technique:

APPLIED	ornament or part applied to the surface.
BELL METAL	is an alloy of copper and tin and has a grey tinge.
BRASS	is an alloy of copper and zinc.
BRITANNIA METAL	resembles silver or polished pewter: the designs are different from those of pewter. Used from about 1790 into the 19th century.
BRITANNIA STANDARD	where the mark of Britannia replaces the sterling mark, used between 1697-1720, indicates 95.8 per cent pure silver.
BRONZE	is an alloy of copper and tin.
CARTOUCHE	is a scrolled or ornate framing for an inscription or pictorial ornament.
CAST	pattern made by running molten metal or pressing soft material into a mould (also the negative mould itself).
CHASING	pushes the metal into pattern without removing any; it is achieved by surface hammering; it is flatter in appearance then engraving. Most brass is chased.
ELECTROPLATE	is similar to Sheffield Plate, rather metallic in appearance, used from mid 19th century. Seams are straight.
EMBOSSING or REPOUSSÉ	are bosses pushed up into patterns from the back.

ENAMELLING   is inlay with a coloured glass-like appearance.

  CHAMPLEVÉ   is a form of enamelling done by cutting out troughs from the metal into which a composition (frit) is melted.

  CLOISONNÉ   is enamelling in which the pattern is defined by a framework of enclosures (cloisons).

ENGINE TURNING   is a mechanical means of decoration, the article turning on a lathe.

ENGRAVING or INCISING   removes the metal by scratching and cutting. Most armorials are engraved, although in the first half of the 18th century some were cast, chased or applied.

EPBM   Electroplated Britannia Metal – post 1850. Only one seam running vertically. Odd parts are sometimes cast of pewter. Makers always stamped their names and catalogue numbers in full, the letters and figures biting into the metal. The copper base sometimes shows through at the seam.

EPGS   Electroplated German Silver.

EPNS   Electroplated Nickel Silver, from about 1840. Recent marks are Crossed Arrows, Crossed Keys, a Bell, a Hand, a Pineapple.

HATCHED   engraved parallel or crossing lines.

NIELLO   engraved lines filled with a black alloy containing lead.

ORMOLU   is gilded bronze, mostly used for mounts.

PEWTER   is an alloy of tin with lead or other grey metal; it has a greyish tinge; it is sometimes polished. There is not always a TOUCH (mark) on pewter and some touches are hard to find (occasionally being inside on the bottom of a vessel). The seam is usually circular. Pewter chalices and small patens may be found in priests' tombs.

     Pewter terminology and shapes differ slightly from those of silver: engraving is 'scratching', a thumb-piece is a 'lever', 'purchase' or 'billet', 'knop' is more usual than knot, 'swan necked' rather than scrolled handle, etc.

RESERVED   is a term used to signify that the surface is left plain (or sometimes hatched) to receive decoration.

SHEFFIELD PLATE   is copper sandwiched between coats of silver. The marks are different from those on silver and in 80 per cent there are no marks; there is seldom a date letter. The seams are crooked.

SILVER PLATE   denotes works in silver which belong to any class other than those of personal ornaments or coins.

SILVERPLATED   is the term used for articles of metal with a thin coating of silver. Different marks from silver.

STERLING STANDARD   shown by the lion passant mark indicates 92.5 per cent pure silver.

WROUGHT   hammered, cut or filed.

It is essential to acquire pocket guides for gold and silver MARKS and pewter touches. Reliance should not be placed on the date letter alone, it should be counterchecked with the maker's mark, style, position of marks and whether they should be subject to wear and tear.

A recording of the above would be
   Silver, London 1969, Wippell Mowbray Church Furnishing Ltd.

The first mark is the MONOGRAM or MAKER'S MARK, the second is the STERLING MARK, the third is the REGISTRATION or TOWN MARK, and the fourth is the DATE LETTER MARK indicating the year of Assay, which is changed annually and varies according to town.

MOST CAREFUL note should be made, not only of the lettering used for the date letter, but also of the shape of the shield or outer silhouette which is sometimes the only recognisable difference.

The placing of the marks on the object should be noted, especially when there is a lid or separate attachment, which might bear different marks.

Most mediaeval chalices were silver gilt.

If the Maker's Mark is not known, a description is necessary; in the above example it could be 'a WM cypher, letters touching one above the other, encompassed by an oval, lion passant in a rectangle, leopard's head in a square, slanting "O" date letter - all shields with clipped corners.'

 The MARKS for Platinum are similar to those for sterling silver, except that 'an orb surmounted by a cross and encompassed by a pentagon' replaces the lion passant or other sterling mark.

The Town Mark remains the same as for silver, i.e. the leopard for London.
The London Date letter mark for 1975 is

The changing MARKS for Gold should be studied: the Standard Mark from 1300 to 1544 was a crowned leopard's head, from 1544 to 1797 a lion passant, from 1798 to 1843 the lion passant denoted 22 carats and a crown denoted 18 carats. From 1844 a crown denoted both 22 and 18 carats and the lower standards now introduced only bore the carat numbers in decimals in addition to the town, date and maker's mark.

FOREIGN PLATE Before 1800 no UK marks were added. From 1842 all imported plate SOLD had to be assayed. From 1883 to 1904 the 'F' mark was added - in a square with chamfered corners for gold, and within a blunt oval for silver. Since 1904 the 'F' punch is omitted, the marking being the appropriate British Hall Marks with the Assay Offices Mark, in square or oval shields as above, plus the decimal value of the standard.

12th and 13th century Norman style CHALICE

Wide shallow bowl with moulded rim, sometimes shallower than in illustration and
with everted rim.

Cylindrical stem, often quite plain.

Spherical knot, either lobed, wrythen
(spiral), plain or pierced.

Circular foot with engraved or raised
ornament and often stamped beading on
the edge (not shown).

19th century CHALICE inspired by Norman
style

Plain conical bowl set in an arcaded calyx,
with filigree decorated architrave and
spandrels, the pillars set with cabochons.

Circular stem annulated with mouldings and
water leaves above and below the angular
knot which is decorated with filigree
scrolling and eight stone bosses.

High circular flaring stepped foot with an
inverted filigree arcade, as in the calyx,
and filigree ornament on the edge.

FONT CUP c.1510

Font-shaped bowl on sturdy trumpet stem
with narrow cabled collet at junction of
bowl and stem.

Bowl annulated by a band, within strapwork,
with raised inscription in Roman capitals,
'COMMUNION CUP', the words separated by
tied scrolls, reserved on a pounced ground,
and probably added in 17th century.

Early 16th century pre-Reformation Tudor
CHALICE

Deep bowl with everted rim, set in star-
shaped calyx.

Hexagonal stem with vertical bands of rope
moulding at each angle.

Gothic knot with six lozenge bosses, each
with a tracery motif reserved on red or
green enamel on the facets, amidst
intervening lobes.

Hexagonal lobed foot with saints in cusped
niches engraved on the panels, one panel
bearing the Crucifixion.

Tudor COMMUNION CUP c.1574

Deep bucket-shaped bowl,
annulated with band of strapwork and
moresques:
resting on a
compressed hemispherical knot above

a wide flange.

Foot and base trumpet-shaped,
with
stamped egg and dart moulding on edge.

Tudor COMMUNION CUP c.1576

Deep beaker-shaped bowl with everted rim
decorated with strapwork arabesques.

Lozenge decorated collet joins bowl and

spool stem with lozenge ornament
at lower edge.

Domed and stepped circular foot, the lower
edge ornamented as on stem, the base
encircled with gadrooning.

COMMUNION CUP c.1600

Deep conical bowl
engraved with IHS across the stem of
a cross, within a rayed frieze.

Baluster stem.

High circular foot stepped at base
with ring moulding.

COMMUNION CUP c.1686

Deep beaker-shaped bowl with everted rim,
engraved with armorials contained within
foliate ornament of two crossed branches
of laurel tied below with a ribbon.
(Inscriptions at this period usually in
English, the lettering as on
contemporary monuments.)

Trumpet-shaped stem with narrow central
flange.
Shallow stepped and domed circular foot.

Mid 18th century COMMUNION CUP

Goblet-shaped bowl girdled with moulding, above which is an engraved IHS within rays and below inverted rays.

Trumpet-shaped stem with compressed moulded knop two-thirds of the way up and engraved putti at the base.

Domed and stepped foot with rayed decoration.

Late 18th century COMMUNION CUP

Ogee-shaped bowl encircled near the top with raised foliate ornament and festoons of flowers and foliage.
Fluted calyx reaching halfway up the bowl.

Baluster stem with spiral gadrooning.

Foliated collet joining the stem to the high domed fluted foot on a spreading base which is encircled with raised acanthus leaves.

Mid 19th century CHALICE

Hemispherical bowl annulated with lines of niello enclosing inscription in 19th century Lombardic. Small cast and applied calyx of fleurs-de-lys. Circular stem with stepped mouldings and vertical wires and pellets on a niello ground. Gadroons and foliated mouldings decorate the knop.
Filigree scrolls on the collet.
Conical foot divided into six panels by rope mouldings each containing an applied roundel with representations of the Evangelists and other symbols.
Stepped circular edge.

20th century CHALICE

Double cone or egg-timer shape, the bowl shallower than the base.

Lower third of bowl and whole stem base decorated with hammered abstract geometrical designs.

CHALICE
showing an amalgamation of decorative details from two silver gilt
chalices of 1525 and 1527.

Hemispherical bowl
annulated with a band inscribed in Gothic lettering
reserved on a hatched ground

    'CALICEM ◇ SALUTARI ◇ ACCIPIUM ◇ ET ◇ NOMEN ◇ INVOCABI' (sic)

Double band of moulding below the bowl.

Hexagonal stem with shafts of twisted wires (cable moulding) on
the angles, the panels in between having tracery devices.

Large Gothic lobular knot with six projecting lozenge
bosses set with raised human masks on the facets.

Wide castellated pierced turret collet at junction of lower part
of stem with high hexagonal foot.

Panels of foot decorated in two stages, the upper with feathering,
the lower with lettering on a hatched ground (indecipherable).

One leaf-shaped panel, protruding from the others, bears an engraved
Crucifixion, the base of the leaf curving onto the bottom step
of a moulded circular stepped flange.

Wavy edged hexagonal stepped base with stamped billet moulding on
the riser.

N.B. Chalices of this period are approximately 17 cm h., those
of similar design made in the 19th or 20th centuries would probably
be larger.

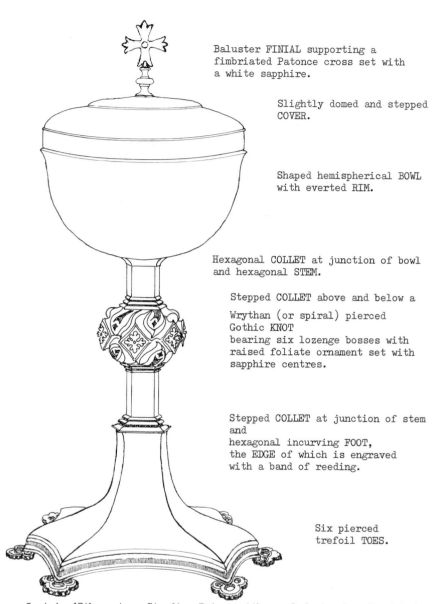

Baluster FINIAL supporting a
fimbriated Patonce cross set with
a white sapphire.

Slightly domed and stepped
COVER.

Shaped hemispherical BOWL
with everted RIM.

Hexagonal COLLET at junction of bowl
and hexagonal STEM.

Stepped COLLET above and below a

Wrythan (or spiral) pierced
Gothic KNOT
bearing six lozenge bosses with
raised foliate ornament set with
sapphire centres.

Stepped COLLET at junction of stem
and
hexagonal incurving FOOT,
the EDGE of which is engraved
with a band of reeding.

Six pierced
trefoil TOES.

Certain 17th century Standing Patens with spool feet, when furnished
with covers, resemble CIBORIUMS, but are known as COVERED PATENS.

The difference between a CIBORIUM, when seen without a cover,
and a CHALICE or CUP, is that the former has a rim or ledge (bezel)
on which the cover rests.

PATEN 12th-14th century

Circular with double depression.
Band contained within the moulded rim
circuminscribed in Latin Lombardic
uncials reserved on a hatched ground:
'+ CALICEM SALUTARIS ACCIPIAM ET
NOMINE DOMINE INVOCABO' with a cross
at the beginning and lozenge devices
between the other words.
The domed centre engraved with a vernicle (Head of Christ) set in a
roundel within an engraved sunburst on a matted ground, all within
an embossed sexfoil with spandrels engraved with small sun motifs.

On the reverse, the Sacred Monogram in Latin form.

STANDING PATEN c.1576
usually made to serve as Cover and Paten
for Communion Cups of the period.
Note the inner rim (bezel) to fit the Cup.

Spool foot, with Button on base, when used
as Paten.

Button engraved horizontally with date in
Roman capitals. Reeded outer edge, as on
top. (Sometimes the Button bears the name
of the church within a roundel set in a
band of the same decoration as on the
outside of the Paten-Lid.)

Spool finial, when used as Cover (lid) for the
cup, the outside annulated with a band of
strapwork and moresques. (Care should be taken
to compare with decoration on accompanying cup.)

So as not to confuse with 'Covered Patens'
(see 'Ciborium') it is safer to call these
PATEN-LIDS rather than 'cover-patens'.

Inside of Paten-Lid undecorated, with single
depression and single-reeded border to narrow
rim, from whence protrudes the fitting edge.

SALVER c.1693 used as PATEN
sometimes wrongly described as a Tazza.

Narrow rim with triple-reeded border. Single depression with
shallow straight-sided bouge. Slight moulded collet at junction
of top and high flaring foot which is edged with ovolo decoration
and stands on a narrow flanged base.
    Incised armorials in centre of well - arms of ....
    London Assay 1693. Maker's Mark 'PM' within a quatrefoil.
    All marks in the well except that of the lion passant which is on
the underside of the flange. Underneath the salver is an incised
'1713'.

N.B. A salver should not be confused with a 'Tazza' which is a
wine-cup with shallow circular bowl, mounted on a foot.

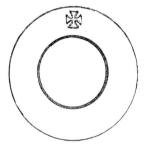

PLATE PATEN

Broad rimmed plate with engraved
patée cross on rim.
Inscription engraved in Roman
capitals on back of rim.

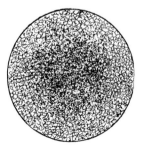

DISH PATEN

Saucer dish with shallow foot-rim.
Hammered decoration covering inside.

Pewter 17th century

Bell-shaped

Brass 17th century

Verticle slot in
cylindrical stem
with protruding
candle ejector

Drip pan in
centre of stem

Wide spreading
base

Silver or Brass
early 18th century

Steel rod ejector
in base

Reel-shaped nozzle
on distinct neck
Shouldered baluster
stem with knops
Moulded and
depressed
polygonal foot

Silver or gilt
late 17th century

Baroque style,
the baluster stem
shaped and orna-
mented, the scrol-
led tripod feet
surmounded by
putti
Gadrooned drip pan
and pricket

Silver
classical style of
Restoration c.1675

Fluted and reeded
column of Doric form
with broad platform
around socket,
mounted on high
waisted plinth
rising from large
square stepped foot

Silver or Brass
neo-classical style
of late 18th
century

Tapering fluted
stem on high
trumpet foot
Bell-shaped leaf
decorated socket

Five-Branch CANDELABRUM

The brass flat-scrolled branches with
ivy leaf repoussé ornament spring from
the top of the cylindrical stem and hold
shallow saucer-shaped grease-pans with
scalloped cresting and annulated
cylindrical nozzles. The central, fifth
socket is at the top of a reeded rod
with scrolling brackets.

A polychrome imbricated iron stem, with
brass terminal ferrule, passes through
the collar of the base and is joined,
by a brass knot, at the top to a brass
cylindrical stem.

The wrought iron tripod base is formed
of broken-scrolled legs with ribbon
ends, united by a wide incurving collar
with bolt-end terminals.

Seven-Branch
JERUSALEM CANDLESTICK
or MEMORAH

PROCESSIONAL TORCH or
BIER LIGHT

in highly polished brass,
135 cm h. to pan.

Removable four-sided
incurving and tapering base
on four bun feet.

Cylindrical stem with two
compressed and stepped knots.

Drip-pan of similar shape to
the base with plain
cylindrical socket.

NOZZLE and

DRIP PAN scalloped, with deep indentations between each pair of scallops, and annulated with two pairs of fillets.

Circular STEM with three KNOTS, the upper one gem set and chased with zigzag ornament, the lower one little more than a flange.
Between them the stem is annulated by double rows of fillets enclosing a zigzag pattern.

Large compressed central KNOT, chased and decorated with bead mouldings and with stones as bosses, the STEM below decorated, as above with fillets and zigzag, and running into

moulded COLLETS above a

high conical FOOT, with, in the upper part, panels formed of chased fillets with stones set in high collets, and in the lower part, pierced cusped openings alternating with pierced roundels.

19th century ALTAR CANDLESTICK
Copper gilt and set with semi-precious stones

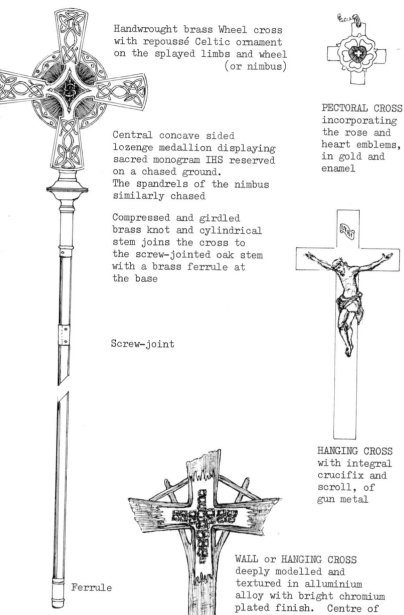

Handwrought brass Wheel cross
with repoussé Celtic ornament
on the splayed limbs and wheel
(or nimbus)

PECTORAL CROSS
incorporating
the rose and
heart emblems,
in gold and
enamel

Central concave sided
lozenge medallion displaying
sacred monogram IHS reserved
on a chased ground.
The spandrels of the nimbus
similarly chased

Compressed and girdled
brass knot and cylindrical
stem joins the cross to
the screw-jointed oak stem
with a brass ferrule at
the base

Screw-joint

HANGING CROSS
with integral
crucifix and
scroll, of
gun metal

WALL or HANGING CROSS
deeply modelled and
textured in alluminium
alloy with bright chromium
plated finish. Centre of
coloured faceted slab glass
set in epoxy resin.
Rustic shape with silhouette.

Ferrule

PROCESSIONAL CROSS
Celtic style

For the names of the
different types of cross
see section on CROSSES

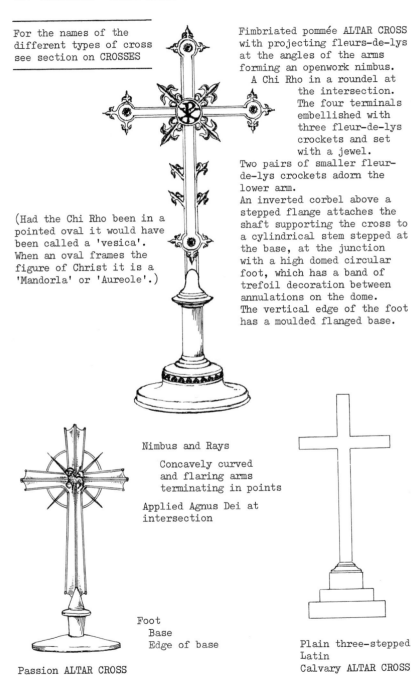

Fimbriated pommée ALTAR CROSS
with projecting fleurs-de-lys
at the angles of the arms
forming an openwork nimbus.
   A Chi Rho in a roundel at
         the intersection.
         The four terminals
         embellished with
         three fleur-de-lys
         crockets and set
         with a jewel.
Two pairs of smaller fleur-
de-lys crockets adorn the
lower arm.
An inverted corbel above a
stepped flange attaches the
shaft supporting the cross to
a cylindrical stem stepped at
the base, at the junction
with a high domed circular
foot, which has a band of
trefoil decoration between
annulations on the dome.
The vertical edge of the foot
has a moulded flanged base.

(Had the Chi Rho been in a
pointed oval it would have
been called a 'vesica'.
When an oval frames the
figure of Christ it is a
'Mandorla' or 'Aureole'.)

Nimbus and Rays

   Concavely curved
   and flaring arms
   terminating in points

Applied Agnus Dei at
intersection

Foot
Base
Edge of base

Passion ALTAR CROSS

Plain three-stepped
Latin
Calvary ALTAR CROSS

ALTAR CROSS with Crucifix

ALTAR CROSS with Crucifix

The arms engraved with fleurs-de-lys in a diaper pattern.
To each arm is attached a quatrefoil edged with roll moulding,
engraved with foliage on a matted ground and set with a single
amethyst.

The three upper arms terminate in fleurs-de-lys with roll mouldings
and engraved foliage centres.

The intersection of the arms, outlined with gables of roll moulding,
but otherwise left plain as a background to the figure of Christ,
is surrounded by an octagon, cusped on its inner side, concave on
its outer and crested on the four exposed angles with fleurs-de-lys,
the width filled with a band of dog-tooth ornament between roll
mouldings on a hatched ground.

(For description of figure see section on CROSSES AND CRUCIFIX.)

An inverted corbel is placed at the junction of the cross and the
knop of the annulated cylindrical stem.

The compressed spherical knop is girdled and has four bosses bearing
applied roundels of fleurs-de-lys reserved on blue enamel.

The high tapering foot is engraved with the Sacred Monogram IHC in a
roundel and a cursive pattern of trefoils, and is edged with four
shaped lobes.

An engraved band of hatching occupies the space between the edge of
the foot and the base.

The wooden frame of the cross is cased on the front in plates of
base metal, the base is of electroplated base metal and the figure
of Christ is electrogilt.

69 cm h.   Made by ... in 1846 (Ref: ....)

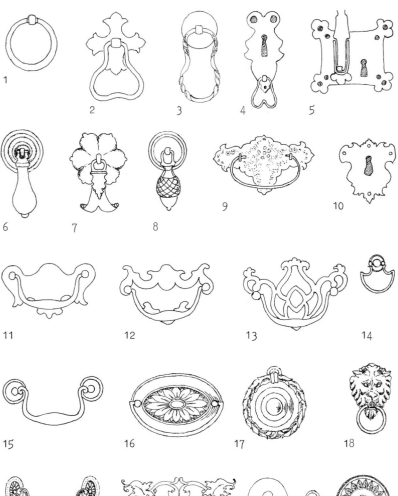

1

2

3

4

5

6

7

8

9

10

11

12

13

14

15

16

17

18

19

20

21

22   23

24

25

26

1   Iron ring

2   Iron loop-drop with cruciform backplate   16th and 17th centuries

3   Iron loop-drop twist with round backplate 16th and 17th centuries

4   Iron heart-shaped loop-drop on a shaped key escutcheon   16th and
    17th centuries

5   Square iron lockplate with trefoil decorated corners   14th and
    15th centuries

6   Cast brass pear-drop on circular moulded backplate   c.1700

7   Split-tail or axe-drop on hexafoil backplate   c.1700

8   Acorn-drop   c.1700

9   Tangs and loop on engraved and shaped backplate   early 18th
    century

10 Shield-shaped key escutcheon, often engraved   early 18th century

11 Bail handle passing through cast knobs on a solid backplate
    c.1710

12 Bail handle passing through cast knobs on a cut-away backplate
    c.1730

13 As above on a pierced backplate   c.1750

14 Dutch-drop   from 1750

15 Swan-necked loop from two circular moulded backplates   from
    1750 and much used in the 19th century

16 Relief-stamped oval backplate with plain loop handle passing
    through two knobs   from c.1770

17 Circular relief-stamped handle on circular moulded backplate
    from c.1770

18 Lion mask with ring   1790-1820

19 Relief-stamped swan-necked handle attached to oval rose-stamped
    backplates

20 Art Nouveau fixed protruding loop   c.1900

21 1740-70

22 1770-

23 Beaded circular loop attached to stamped circular backplate
    c.1820

24 Mid 18th century Chinese style with geometric piercing

25 Rococo from c.1750 with two separate plates for handle sockets,
    sometimes with asymmetrical decoration: earlier examples would
    have a single backplate

26 Sunken or Recessed handle as found on military chests   c.1820

Although dates have been given for the above, all have been much
copied.

Solid Barrel
or Bolt End
and Open Scarf
Collar

Flat Nib or
Half-penny Snub
and Astragal
Collar

Fiddlehead and
Clip Collars

Rolled Nib

Many others not illustrated

13th and 14th
century
stamped
tendril
ornament

17th and 18th
century
wrought iron
waterleaf

17th and 18th
century
repoussée sheet
iron acanthus

18th century
cast iron
medallion

Fish Tail

Twist

Ribbon End

Ribbon End
Scroll

Scrolls

Tapering metal SCREWS were first used in the late 17th century and
were hand-filed with irregular thread. Lathe-turned screws appeared
in the late 18th century, and machine-made screws in the mid 19th
century.

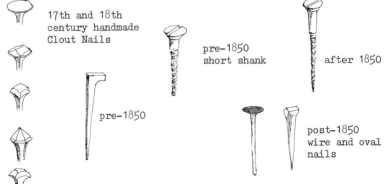

17th and 18th
century handmade
Clout Nails

pre-1850
short shank

after 1850

pre-1850

post-1850
wire and oval
nails

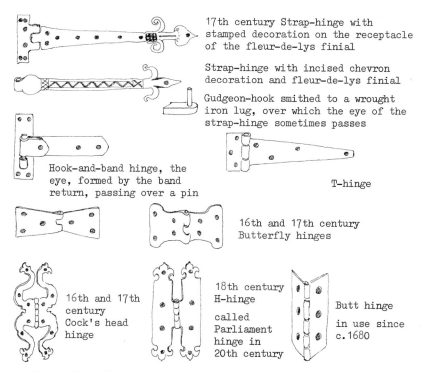

17th century Strap-hinge with stamped decoration on the receptacle of the fleur-de-lys finial

Strap-hinge with incised chevron decoration and fleur-de-lys finial

Gudgeon-hook smithed to a wrought iron lug, over which the eye of the strap-hinge sometimes passes

Hook-and-band hinge, the eye, formed by the band return, passing over a pin

T-hinge

16th and 17th century Butterfly hinges

16th and 17th century Cock's head hinge

18th century H-hinge

called Parliament hinge in 20th century

Butt hinge

in use since c.1680

The earliest Norman hinges recall Viking designs, being usually crescent-shaped with snake-head, tendril or flower terminals. 12th century hinges are more geometrical.

The 13th century was the period of the 'Great Hinge' - the scrollwork period. In the 14th century the art of the Smith declined: see WOODWORK.

Dating is difficult, as all were copied in the 19th and 20th centuries, although neither the wispiness nor the crudeness of the stampwork was ever reproduced.

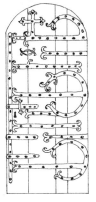
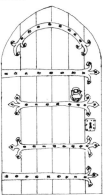

Bow

S
h
a
n
k

Bit

14th
century
with simple
bow, plain
shank and
thin bit with
parallel
sides

Late 18th
century
for Tumbler
bit latch

18th cen-
tury with
pierced
bow

18th century 19th century
Cabinet keys

Pre-1850 keys usually have the bits filed
on the front;   after 1850 they are filed
on the bottom edge.

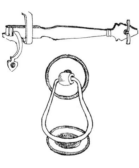

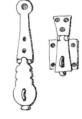

Hinged iron
Strap-lock
and staple
to secure a font cover

Hasps and
Staples

Old Stock Lock and
latch with a heavy wood
casing containing a
bolt operated by a key

16th century
iron lock-plate

Escutcheon
lift-hatch

Suffolk latch and
turning Knocker latch
handle for same

Hatchet-shaped
latch with Tumbler
bit latch lock

Suffolk or
Norfolk latch
with grasp handle

Hold-back catch for gates

Brass LECTERN c.1683

Book desk in form of an eagle
with outstretched wings
flanked by single bracket
candle holders with glass tulip-
shaped shades, standing on

a sphere

which is supported on a
flaring concave section above
various bands of moulding including
some raised leaf work.

Baluster stem
with
a stepped circular base above

a cylindrical section
springing
from more stepped moulding above
the high-domed lectern base which
rests on four lion séjant feet.

Brass Lecterns prior to 19th century are
usually very austere and made up of many
parts slotted together.

Brass LECTERN late 19th century with
restored iron feet

Double desk, the gable ends pierced
with cusped circular openings, a band
of cresting across the top, the side
edges of the book-stops daggered.
Circular stem decorated with rings of
red and blue inlaid mastic, with at
the top formalised leaf forms
supporting the desk.
Central compressed spherical knot with
an attached band with knobbed
decoration and scalloped edges, and
trefoil collets above and below.
A similar collet at junction of stem
and conical base which is decorated
with pierced sexfoils and rings of red
and blue inlaid mastic and stands on
four red-painted paw feet protruding
from the cusped edge.

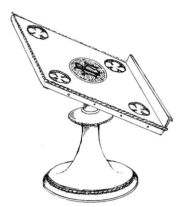

Pedestal type MISSAL STAND
in highly polished brass
with revolving bookplate
embellished with pierced
quatrefoils within roundels
in the corners and a central
roundel with IHC in Latin form
reserved on a punched ground.

Rope moulded edging to bookplate,
screw joint and trumpet base.

Ledger type MISSAL STAND
with scrolled and foliated
end panels and scalloped edge
to bookplate ledge.

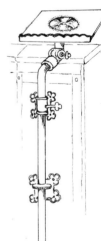

PULPIT DESK
with quatrefoil decoration in
centre and a scalloped ledge.
The stem, adjustable, by use of
a key, is attached to the inside
of the pulpit drum by clips to
square bracket plates which have
trefoil corners.

Brass CHANDELIER of mixed periods

Basically a chandelier is composed of a central shaft of ball and baluster turnings, two or three tiers of curving arms (branches) springing from the shaft, a top finial and a pendant finial.
The central parts are hollow and held together by an iron hanging rod.

Descriptions should include the shape and ornamentation of ALL the parts and the ways they are fitted, the number of tiers and the number of branches on each, the pendant finial, and, most important, the finial between the hanging ring and stem.

The finial illustrated is known as a 'London Dove' – a 'Bristol Dove' would have the wings close and no feathers on the body. Provincial centres had their own characteristic finials.

17th century chandeliers have the arms hooked into rings in the balusters or sometimes into trays pierced with holes, their length causing them to droop. English designs are plainer than those that came from Holland at this time. The branches are mostly circular in section and are of two opposed curves with moulding at the join, the inner end is an open spiral, the outer end everted.

During the 18th century the arms became shorter, drooped less and were fitted to the circumference of the spheres (globe collar) which itself became flatter. The branches were more elaborate, often hexagonal or octagonal in section and covered with scrolling; the wide spaces between branches and tiers were filled with ornament, mostly gadrooning. The most favoured finial was a flame.

Those from Holland, at this period, were without finial or ornament and the branches were attached by tenons and pins, instead of hooks, to hollow trays.

Manufacture ceased in England during the 19th century.

BIBLIOGRAPHY

RAMSEY, L.G.G. (ed.) (1962), 'The Complete Encyclopaedia of Antiques', The Connoisseur, London.

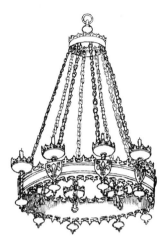

Wrought iron CORONA LUCIS

hanging by chains from a circlet
crested with fleurs-de-lys; the bowl
drip-pans under the eight candle
sockets similarly ornamented and
attached to the outer side of the
coronet by twist stems with pendant
turnip-shaped finials, the joins
hidden by applied fleur-de-lys
decorated shields, painted red and
gold. The rims of the annulated
coronet decorated with fleurs-de-lys.

SANCTUARY LAMP

in highly polished brass with cast and
finely modelled Dolphin arms attached by
their tails to a ball and baluster pendant
finial of the drip-pan, by their snouts to
the socket in which an eight day type ruby
glass cylindrical funnel with everted lip
rests, and by their dorsal fins to three
chains hanging from a brass circlet
surmounted with a ring similar to that at
the base of the pendant finial.

PROCESSIONAL TORCH

in chromium
plated brass on
teak stem,
with clear
glass cylin-
drical funnel.
A handle-grip
of textured brass
prevents it
slipping through
the collar of the
wall mounted bracket.

SANCTUARY BRACKET LAMP

in bright polished
chromium plate with
glass funnel nestling
in a calyx above a disc
set on a flaring reeded
stem which sits in a
collar at the end of a
shaped triangular wall
bracket.

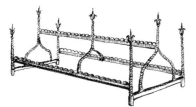

Wrought iron HERSE 14th century
erected around or above
some tombs for their
protection, with fleur-de-lys
decorated prickets for candles.

19th century wrought iron PORCH LANTERN of
hexagonal shape.

The tapering glazed panels have iron traceried
glazing bars in their heads; the edge of the
upper rail to which they are fixed is scrolled-
over and crested with a band of pierced arcading
between the scroll and a similarly scrolled-over
lower edge of the double-domed cover.
Both sections of the cover have ogee ribs and
scrolled-over lower edges: the panels are
pierced, with whorls in the lower and lozenges
in the upper section: between the two sections
is a band with rectangular piercing.
Baluster finial to which a ring is attached.
At the base of the lantern is a pendant finial
of scrolled brackets radiating from the centre
to the plain moulded outside edges of the bottom
rail of the glazed panels.

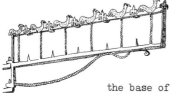

16th century wrought iron bracket
of PRICKETS, attached to wall and
pivoted.
Two horizontal bars, connected by
spiral uprights, form five open
panels with a spike at midpoint of
the base of each as support for a candle which
passes through a ring in the upper bar
that is crested with alternating
fleurs-de-lys and cocks.

CRESSET STONE   STRAP SCONCE   RUSHLIGHT HOLDER

Brass bracket GASOLIER

with a band of floral engraving on
the globe which sits in a trefoil
crested socket with acorn pendant
finial.
The waterleaf-decorated scrolled arm
has a cast brass fleurette inner
terminal to the scroll-end nearest the
wall plate, which end is linked to one
of the waterleaves.

Brass candle SCONCE

of cartouche shape with repoussé
decoration and bearing an un-
inscribed cartouche in the centre.
The lower part is reeded and fluted.
A simple, knotted, S-shaped arm of
round section springs from a
floriated boss at the base of the
sconce and holds a plain saucer-shaped
drip-pan with annulated cylindrical
nozzle moulded at the rim.

Brass candle BRACKET

A horizontal rod of square section
interrupted by twists, emerges from
a fleurette on the backplate and is
supported above and below by inward
scrolling waterleaf brackets, and
terminates in a trefoil.
Near the terminal is a floral collar
through which is threaded the stem of
an urn-shaped socket.

Hanging GAS LAMP

with clear glass chimney and opaque
china hemispherical cover.
The brass body fits into an annulated
iron girdle to which are attached
three wrought iron broken-scrolled
brackets which are themselves
suspended from iron linked chains.

ALMS DISH or BASIN - a large plate, usually of base metal and mostly over 30 cm diameter.

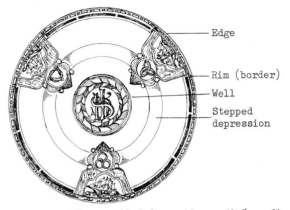

Edge

Rim (border)

Well

Stepped depression

Silver with enamelled decoration.   40.5 cm diameter overall.
Circular, with moulded and patterned edge to the panelled rim.
Three medallions rise from bosses from the stepped depression of the dish, containing embossed representations of the Holy Trinity - Triquetra, Circle within Triangle and Interwoven Circles - they are framed by enamelled wing forms arching back to the rim, and framing, on the rim, silver reliefs of sailing ships.
In the centre of the dish, The Sacred Monogram IHS reserved in an enamelled roundel within coiled rope pattern.

PAX

A tablet with a projecting handle behind, usually decorated on the front with a Rood or sacred symbol.

PYX

A vessel to carry the Sacrament to the sick. Usually a box similar to, though smaller than, a wafer box, but sometimes in other forms, even resembling a chalice.

WAFER BOX with lift-out grid

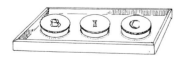

CHRISTOMATORY containing a Set of HOLY OIL STOCKS

A TABERNACLE is a repository in which the Pyx may be safely placed.

ALTAR TABERNACLE
in three stages, each of
which can be separately described
(see description of a Font Cover in
WOODWORK).

Lower stage, square in plan, each
side with a crocketed gable, on
the front a door decorated with
a raised cross ... etc.
Second stage open (in order to
accommodate the Monstrance
at Exposition) with buttresses
supporting an hexagonal gabled
canopy.
Third stage, a pinnacled
and crocketed spirelet.

HANGING TABERNACLE
with Veil

FLOWERSTAND
adapted from a
TORCHÈRE

Disc top with embattled
gallery.
Section of twist stem
joined by a spindle
collet to a rectangular
section supported by
scrolled cruciform
bracket feet united to
the stem by clip collars
in three places.

PORTABLE FONT

Oak with hand-forged
wrought iron cruciform
standard on oak plinth
with chamfered edges.
Metal lift-out bowl.
Cercelée cross iron
finial on lid.

BAPTISMAL SHELL

with shaped silver
handle on which is
an engraved Maltese
cross.

Silver STOUP or Holy Water Basin,
usually near the entrance to a church
and more often made of stone.

The backplate of the one illustrated is of
lozenge-shaped cartouche form and has
strapwork, repoussé and hammered decoration,
with the Sacred Monogram superimposed on a
Latin cross reserved on a central medallion.
The acanthus decorated bombé basin is
stepped at the base and has a pendant ball
and steeple finial.

Silver ASPERGES BUCKET

Shaped body in two stages;   the upper with
a moulded and floriated rim is double-curved;
the lower vase-shaped with chased decoration
of a cupid head and festoons.   Collet at
junction of body and foot.   High domed foot
with a turned-over edge and matted and
scrolled decoration.
Tubular lobed bale or swing-handle.

ASPERGES or Holy Water Sprinkler

with perforated ball finial and
baluster stem of silver, attached
to an oak handle with silver
baluster knop.

INCENSE BOAT of canoe shape, c.1742

edged with a roll moulding, on a baluster
stem above a high circular foot stepped
at the base.
Double lid, hinged amidship, the ends of
the flaps secured by cast scrolled clasps
projecting from the bulwarks.

'Stem-struck' STRAINER SPOON
of Old English pattern c.1730
with elliptical bowl. Name of
church engraved in script on end.

PASTORAL STAFF or CROZIER

Silver-gilt, decorated with enamels and
semi-precious stones.
Maker's mark (above niches) F:C
London 1890 (Ref: Victoria & Albert
Museum Catalogue, 1971, p.124)
Total height 180 cm

Hexagonal crook, imbricated and set with stones,
terminating in a serpent's head with forked tongue.
The curve is connected to the stem by foliated
ornament in the centre, the figures of Christ
charging St Peter, the former standing, the latter
seated, on an enamelled ground.
Flanking the stem are two tiers of niches,
separated by pinnacled buttresses, occupied by
figures of saints and bishops under foliated
canopies; the upper tier is surmounted by three
more figures standing against alternate facets
of the hexagonal stem.
The plinth of the lower tier of niches is set on a
foliated boss rising, by a concave stem, from a
knot decorated with swirling gadroons.
A shield, bearing the arms of the See, is set on
the ferrule at the top of the oak staff.

CHURCH WARDEN'S WAND (usually screw-jointed)
and the shorter VERGER'S WAND

Various finials are applied to the wands:
those illustrated should not be confused
with a Cross-Staff which may precede an
Archbishop, together with his Pastoral
Staff (152 cm and jointless).

Finial

Collet

Ferrule

CANDLE EXTINGUISHER
and TAPER

Stem

Hinged retaining clip

Both the brass
cone-shaped
extinguisher with
rolled edge and
patée cross finial
and the bent
cylindrical taper
holder are
attached by a
brass ferrule to
the oak stem.

Ferrule

MONSTRANCE

Silver, parcel-gilt and set with carbuncles,
in the form of a shrine,
with a glazed crested roundel in the
centre front, edged with rope moulding and
fleurs-de-lys tracery, supported on a
stepped silver plinth with gilt moulding,
engraved dog-tooth patterning and set with
five carbuncles.
On each side, a buttress decorated with
tracery and geometric patterns, pinnacled
and crocketed, with niches in which are two
gilt figures of angels holding crowns.
Above the roundel, a gabled silver roof
engraved with a sexfoil foliated device,
set with carbuncles, and with gilt cresting.
A floriated gilt cross, with a central
carbuncle, rises from dormers.
The shrine rests on an hexagonal stem
decorated with engraved dog-tooth and other
ornament, branching at its top into scrolls
and crockets and edged horizontally with
brattishing.
Compressed spherical knot with embossed
lobes and six bosses, each framed in
swirling crockets and set with a carbuncle.
Gilt collet at junction of stem and foot.
Hexfoil foot, parcel-gilt, decorated with
foliated ornament on a matted ground, set
with a carbuncle in each foil; the base
with gilt mouldings and engraved decoration.
Birmingham, 1848.
Maker's mark of John Hardman & Co.
(Ref: Victoria & Albert Museum Catalogue,
1971, B.19.)

CENSER

Lobed hexagonal body with everted edge.
To each lobe is applied a roundel,
cusped inside with a spoke pattern
ending in trefoils.
Hexagonal foot with double roll edge,
each facet being pierced with a hole for
an attachment.
Domed and stepped cover with lobed rim,
decorated with double roll mouldings, the
dome with pierced dormers.
The finial encased in a cresting of
loops, through which run three chains
rising from attachments on the base.
Thumbpiece attached to a trefoil base.

Overthrow made up of two large
bifurcated 'S' scrolls, passing
through a collar at the centre and
decorated with small scrolls which
include 'fiddlehead' and flat 'penny'
nibs and a pair of well placed
waterleaves.
Below the cornice of the overthrow
is a frieze of strapwork between two
square section rails, similar to the
panel in the double lockrail.

The top and bottom rails are of plain
square section, the bottom rail
carrying a dograil of arrowheads.

In each gate there are four square
section verticals, between the
unadorned stiles, the verticles being
morticed and tennoned and welded through
the horizontals.

Pair of 17th century wrought iron GATES

16th century wrought iron Tomb Railing
of fleur-de-lys alternating with spiked
finials to the arrassed uprights which
change into the flat above the toprail.

The main verticals, with ball and
steeple finials, are ornamented with a
double bar twist below the toprail.

MORSE sewn or pinned onto a band joining the
sides of the Cope (see VESTMENTS):
sometimes embroidered, but usually of
metal.

The illustration shows The Trinity in
basse-taille enamel on silver with a
pierced gold outer rim.

Ramshorn
or Corkscrew

Volute

FINIALS or TERMINALS
at base of handles

Note that in Ceramics
they are termed
'KICK-BACKS'.

Rat tail

Scroll

Moulded

Fish tail

Chair

Bifurcated
Kidney

Heel

Open

Pierced

Spade

Pomegranate

Bud

Ball

Attention

Hammerhead

Embryo shell

Shield

Bifurcated
leaf

Bifurcated

Leaf

Scroll

Charles I Silver FLAGON

Beefeater (or flat cap) lid with moulded thumbpiece pierced with a heart motif.

Tall cylindrical body with boldly cast lip.

Hollow scroll handle of tapering form with simple shield-shaped finial.

Spreading skirt foot with moulded band above.

Body engraved at the front with armorials (...) and inscription (...) in contemporary script.

27.5 cm h.   London Assay 1638. Marks on upper part of body towards handle.
Maker's Mark PD pellets above.

A FLAGON is a large vessel from which other vessels are filled.

A TANKARD is a drinking vessel with a handle and detachable lid.

A MUG is similar to a tankard but without a cover and is sometimes called a CUP.

A BEAKER is usually more shaped and lipped than a mug and without a handle.

Charles II tapering cylindrical pewter TANKARD

Reeded flat-topped raised cover with rim extended in front and edge serrated. Corkscrew thumbpiece, swan-necked handle with applied rat-tail terminal. Applied girdle where base of handle meets the raised body and above which is wriggled decoration.
Narrow, slightly convex, moulded reeded base.

N.B. 'Swan-necked' is more often used in pewter terminology than 'scrolled'.

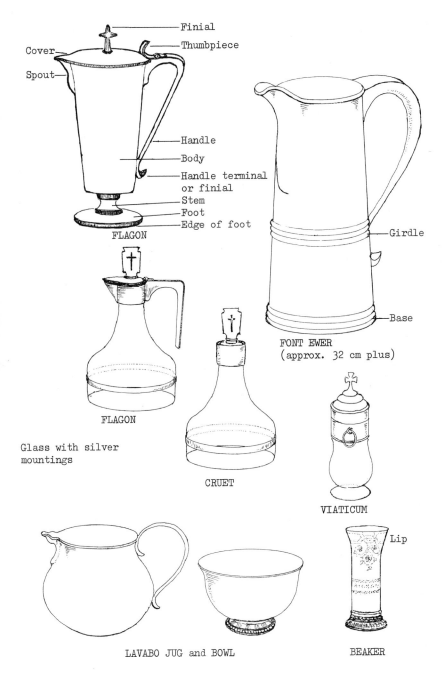

Finial

Thumbpiece

Cover

Spout

Handle

Body

Handle terminal
or finial

Stem

Foot

Edge of foot

FLAGON

Girdle

Base

FONT EWER
(approx. 32 cm plus)

FLAGON

Glass with silver
mountings

CRUET

VIATICUM

Lip

LAVABO JUG and BOWL

BEAKER

19th century FLAGON
with pear-shaped ruby glass body and electrogilt metal mounts

High domed MOUNT, attached to the hinged COVER that has a
trefoil THUMBPIECE, is decorated with a row of tracery edged
with rope moulding and a CRESTING of trefoils surrounding a
wire-work nest, on which sits a 'Pelican in her Piety'.

Plain LIP, triangular in section, projects from a band of
engraved vine ornament.

Scroll HANDLE with mouchette tracery in the ROUNDEL and a
bifurcated TERMINAL.

UPPER MOUNT annulated with a roll moulding and pendant cut-card
fleurs-de-lys, with above, a FRIEZE of quatrefoil tracery
surmounted by the inscription 'Christ so loved us' which is
enclosed by roll mouldings and reserved on a hatched ground
and engraved in Roman capitals.

Engraved metal ROUNDEL, edged with cut-card trefoils and
enclosing the Sacred Monogram, on the front of the glass body
between the MOUNTS which encase the upper and lower parts.

LOWER MOUNT annulated with a roll moulding and surmounted by
cut-card fleurs-de-lys.

High quatrefoil FOOT with moulded edge, is engraved with crosses
within roundels, hatched as for the inscription.

Unmarked: made by John Hardman & Co.
(Ref: Victoria & Albert Museum Catalogue, 1971, B.20.)

BIBLIOGRAPHY

BANISTER, J. (1965), 'English Silver', Ward Lock, London.
BRADBURY, F. (1964), 'Guide to Marks of Origin on British and Irish Silver Plate ....', J.W. Northend, Sheffield (a useful pocket guide).
BURY, S. (1971), 'Victorian Electroplate', Hamlyn, London.
COTTERELL, H. (1929), 'Old Pewter its Makers and Marks', Batsford, London.
HOLLISTER-SHORT, G.J. (1970), 'Discovering Wrought Iron', Shire Publications, Aylesbury.
HUGHES, G.B. (1963), 'The Country Life Collector's Pocket Book', Hamlyn, London.
JACKSON, SIR C.J. (1921), 'English Goldsmiths and Their Marks', Dover, Colchester.
LINDSAY, J.S. (1964), 'Anatomy of English Wrought Iron', Alec Tiranti, London.
McKAY, W.B. (1946), 'Joinery', Longman, London.
OMAN, C.C. (1968), 'English Church Plate 597-1830', O.H.P. Black, London.
PEAL, C.A. (1971), 'Old Pewter and Britannia Metal', John Giffard, London.
RAMSEY, L.G.G. (1962), 'The Complete Encyclopaedia of Antiques', The Connoisseur, London.
TAYLOR, G. (1956), 'Silver', Penguin, Harmondsworth.
VICTORIA & ALBERT MUSEUM (1971) Catalogue of 'Victorian Church Art'.
WIPPELL MOWBRAY (1974) Catalogue 296/74 'Churchcrafts' (recommended for beginners only).

Great help in describing Church Plate may be obtained from County Records similar to 'The Church Plate of Oxfordshire' by J.T. Evans, published by the Alden Press, Oxford, 1928.

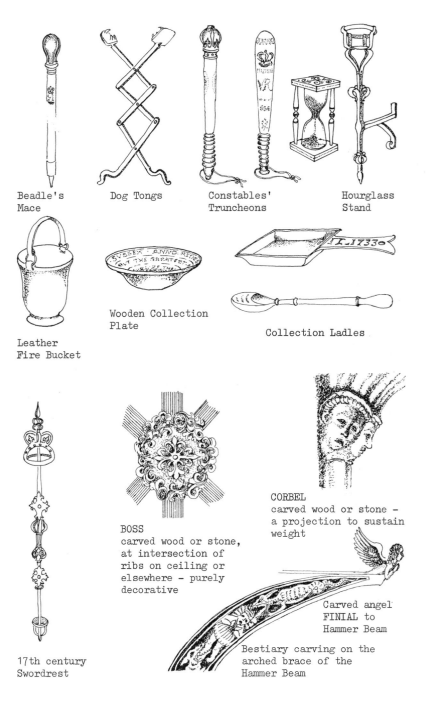

Beadle's
Mace

Dog Tongs

Constables'
Truncheons

Hourglass
Stand

Leather
Fire Bucket

Wooden Collection
Plate

Collection Ladles

17th century
Swordrest

BOSS
carved wood or stone,
at intersection of
ribs on ceiling or
elsewhere - purely
decorative

CORBEL
carved wood or stone -
a projection to sustain
weight

Carved angel
FINIAL to
Hammer Beam

Bestiary carving on the
arched brace of the
Hammer Beam

(sic) ..... in brackets after a word or expression shows that it is quoted exactly though its incorrectness would suggest that it was not.

POLYCHROME ..... many colours.

MURAL ..... the use of 'mural' should be reserved for wall paintings in a church.

WOODS ..... even museum experts are not always able to recognise the different woods.

MEASUREMENTS ..... should never give rise to doubt. An overall measurement should always be given as well as bits and pieces. The format should be consistently height x width x depth. If the height of a column is given 'to the capital' it should be made clear whether that infers to the base of the capital or its top.

KNOP ..... described in 'Oxford Dictionary' as a knob or bud of flower.

KNOT ..... described in 'Oxford Dictionary' as a lump and as an excrescence in stem, branch or root.

However, the terms appear to be interchangeable!

JEWELLERY

Cabochons are stones of rounded, natural form, polished but not cut. Cameos are cut in relief. Intaglios are gems with incised design. Girandoles are openwork clasps of alternating ribbon and bow design, set with stones. Filigree is gold wire or pellets applied to gold (or silver) base in ornamental pattern. A Facet is one side of a cut gem. Jewels set in 19th and 20th century church plate are likely to be facetted, whereas earlier gems are usually cabochon.

ARCHITECTURAL PLANS are of the greatest importance. All details of architect, date, scale, etc. should be given.

PHOTOGRAPHS have not always been carefully preserved - include all those found, even if screwed up at the back of a cupboard, and record the name of the sitter, the date, the photographer and printer and whether signed.

MODELS Some churches contain models made to the order of the architect: these are vitally important and should be carefully noted and distinguished from those more recently made.

The Church Leaflet and County Reference Books usually give a full
description of the BELLS, but consultation with the Bell Captain is
advised as well as perusal of accounts and minutes as there may
have been alterations since the records were made.

It should be noted that Hanging Chambers sometimes have an
affinity to elephant traps, bells are 'feminine' and the name of the
team that rings is the St ... Tower.

The character of the lettering and the Foundry Marks upon old
bells, are of great assistance in determining their date, although
the STAMPS were used for centuries and sometimes different founders
used the same stamps simultaneously.

See section on LETTERING for the difference between Lombardic,
Black Letter or Roman.

The information required is the name or number of each bell,
the note,
the weight,
the inscription with above details,
the date if not given in the
inscription,
by whom rehung and when.

The chief Bell Foundries in England:

John of York 14th century
Samuel Smith (father and son) of York 1680-1730
Abraham Rudhall of Gloucester 1684-1774
Mot 16th century
Lester & Pack c.1750
Christopher Hodson of London c.1681
Richard Phelps c.1716
Whitechapel Bell Foundry (now Mears & Stainbank)
Warner & Sons of Spitalfields
Taylor & Co. of Loughborough

BIBLIOGRAPHY

COCKS, A.H. (1897), 'The Church Bells of Buckinghamshire', Jarrold,
London.
'Encyclopaedia Britannica'.

COINS   Expert advice should be sought for any coins found and if possible a rubbing taken.

       The side showing the monarch's head is the OBVERSE, the other side being the REVERSE.

MAPS   Dates, often hidden in the decoration, may be misleading and study of authentic specimens may help the recorder to recognise the different qualities of hand-made paper, contemporary watermarks, cartography symbols, title treatment and colouring tones. The obvious details, not forgetting the scale, should be given.

MEDALS   are circular and of metal and have obverse and reverse sides: they are commemorative of persons or events.

PRINTS   Recorders should learn to recognise the three main types:

    INTAGLIO   which include line, steel, stipple, engraving, etching, dry point and acquatint.

    RELIEVO   woodcuts and wood engravings.

    PLANOGRAPHIC   another name for Lithography which resembles drawing made with a very soft pencil.

The simplest of the DEFINITIONS are:

LAID DOWN	prints pasted on paper.
ORIGINAL ENGRAVING	engraving by the artist.
PROOF	signed by artist and engraver.
PROOF BEFORE LETTERS	unsigned, the name of the artist and engraver printed.
LETTERED PROOF	Title of Subject, names of artist, engraver and publisher printed.

The technical terms used in the lettering are mostly in Latin or French, with abbreviations and contemporary spelling.

Dileneavit, figuravit, dessiné ...	drawn by
Incidit, sculpsit, fecit ...	engraved by
Composuit ...	designed by
Excudit, formit ...	printed by
Pinxit, peint à la guasche ...	painted by

STAMPS   are more valuable when attached to envelopes and many are to be found amongst the faculties and correspondence in the church records. Note should be made of the dates.

BIBLIOGRAPHY

HUGHES, C.B. (1963), 'The Country Life Collector's Pocket Book', Hamlyn, London.
'Seaby's Coins of England and the U.K.', B.A. Seaby Ltd, London.
WHITTINGTON-EGAN, R. (1968), 'Pocket Money Guide', Drive Publications, London.

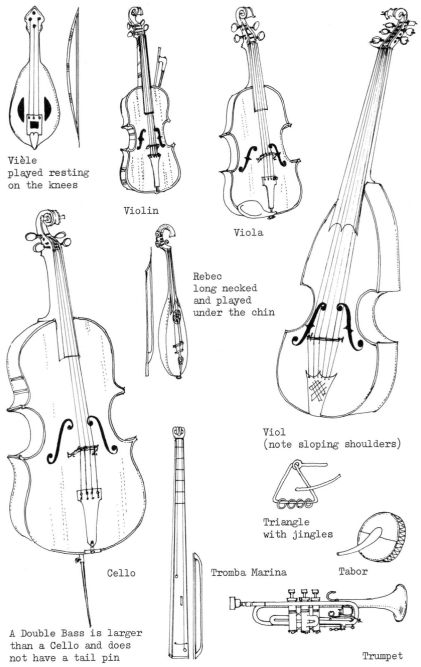

Vièle
played resting
on the knees

Violin

Viola

Rebec
long necked
and played
under the chin

Cello

A Double Bass is larger
than a Cello and does
not have a tail pin

Viol
(note sloping shoulders)

Triangle
with jingles

Tromba Marina

Tabor

Trumpet

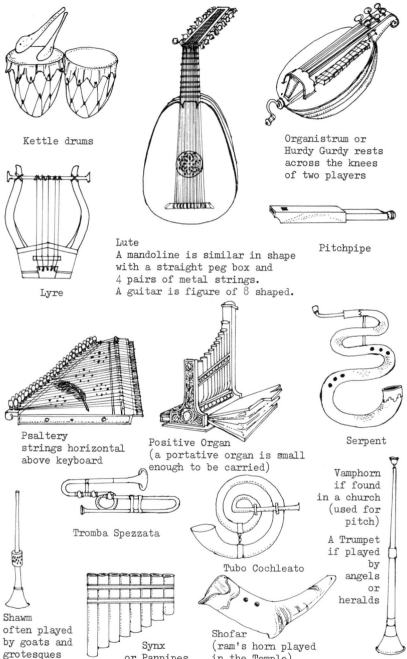

Kettle drums

Lyre

Lute
A mandoline is similar in shape
with a straight peg box and
4 pairs of metal strings.
A guitar is figure of 8 shaped.

Organistrum or
Hurdy Gurdy rests
across the knees
of two players

Pitchpipe

Psaltery
strings horizontal
above keyboard

Positive Organ
(a portative organ is small
enough to be carried)

Serpent

Tromba Spezzata

Tubo Cochleato

Vamphorn
if found
in a church
(used for
pitch)

A Trumpet
if played
by
angels
or
heralds

Shawm
often played
by goats and
grotesques

Synx
or Panpipes

Shofar
(ram's horn played
in the Temple)

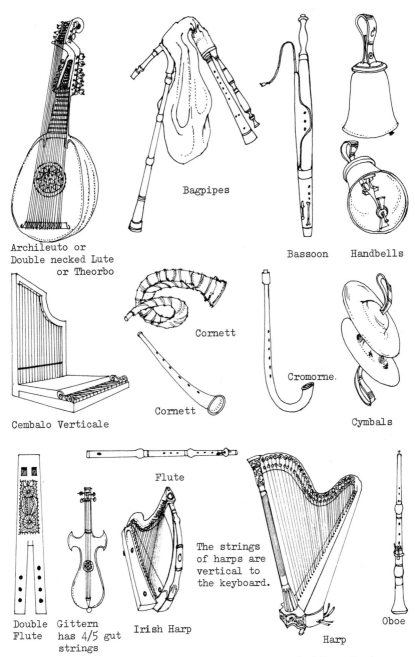

Archileuto or
Double necked Lute
or Theorbo

Bagpipes

Bassoon   Handbells

Cembalo Verticale

Cornett

Cornett

Cromorne.

Cymbals

Flute

Double   Gittern
Flute   has 4/5 gut
         strings

Irish Harp

The strings
of harps are
vertical to
the keyboard.

Harp

Oboe

A Cittern is fig-shaped, the metal strings played with a plectrum.

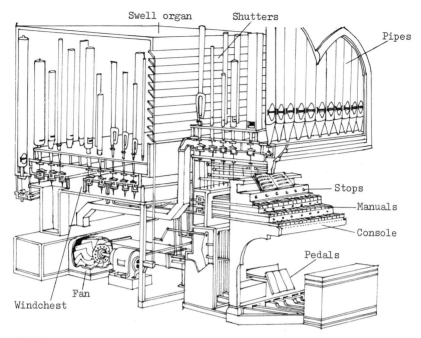

ORGAN

The Puritans destroyed most of the organs in England and few are to
be found earlier than mid 19th century. A few churches have an old
Barrel Organ.

An organ CASE (enclosing the works and pipes) is sometimes a
thing of beauty and should be described as for a piece of furniture
with the measurements given.

The part where the player sits is called a CONSOLE and contains
from one to five keyboards for the hands (MANUALS), and a keyboard
for the feet (PEDALS), and a section of STOPS, usually white with
the names and measurements (in feet) painted on them, possibly in
German, French, Italian or Latin.

The Manuals, each of which is a complete organ in itself, are
named Great, Choir, Swell, Solo, Pedal or Echo.

The Pipes, metal or wood, are contained in the 'Upper Board'.

The Wind is stored in Bellows and conveyed through a wind-trunk
into a windchest, either electrically or by hand or foot.

The information of most use is

1 Name of Builder and date of installation which is often to be
   found on a label on the console.
2 Particulars of enlargement or restoration and maintenance and
   the name of the donor.
3 Description of the console and case-work.
4 Whereabouts of the Specification.

HARMONIUMS and AMERICAN ORGANS – invented in 1840 and found in churches, the essential difference between them being in the direction of the current of air. They have a keyboard of five octaves and are described in the 'Encyclopaedia Britannica' (1911) as wind keyboard instruments, small organs without pipes, furnished with free reeds.

ELECTRONIC ORGANS – the most widely-known maker being the Hammond Company of America.

AUTOMATIC PIANO PLAYERS, with perforated rolls, first appeared c.1842.

PIANOS – grand (horizontal), upright, cottage (small upright).

The 'trade label' or name of maker is important, the best-known amongst Grand and mini-grands are Érard, Broadwood, Bechstein, Joseph Smith, Steinway, Silberman and Clementi.

The first 'Cottage' or upright pianos, using iron framing, independent of the case, were made by John Isaac Hawkins in 1800. Other names associated with cottage pianos are Southwell, Robert Wornum, William Allen, Stodart, Alphaeus Babcock, Conrad Meyer and Jonas Chickering.

Pianos may be described as for a piece of furniture but it should be clear whether the measurements given are of the inside or outside.

BIBLIOGRAPHY

CLUTTON, C. and NILAND, A. (1963), 'The British Organ', Batsford, London.
HARRISON, F. and RIMMER, J. (1964), 'European Musical Instruments', Studio Vista, London.
HINDLEY, G. (1971), 'Musical Instruments', Hamlyn, London.

2 Calves - King Walstan, who also holds a scythe
1 Cow - St Bridget
1 Dog - Roch, with wound in leg
2 Dogs - Dominic, with black and white dogs holding torches in
       mouths
Dragon - George, usually in armour - not to be confused with arch-
       angel Michael who also has a dragon, also Martha
Dragon and cross - Margaret of Antioch
Dragon led by chain - Juliana
Hog - Anthony
Horse, white - George
Lamb - Agnes, Francis of Assisi, John the Baptist
Lion - Adrian or Euphemia or Jerome
Lion, winged - Mark
Lion and Raven - Vincent
Mule, kneeling - Anthony of Padua
Otter - Cuthbert (Bishop)
Ox, winged - Luke
Pig, Boar or Hog - Anthony of Egypt
Sheep - Genevieve
Stag - Adrian or Eustace or Hubert
Wolf, guarding his head - King Edmund
Wolf, Lion or Cock - Vitus

Man, winged - Matthew

Birds - Francis of Assisi
Cock - Peter
Cock, Lion or Wolf - Vitus
Dove on sceptre - King Edmund
Dove - Pope Gregory
Dove on shoulder - David of Wales (Bishop)
2 Doves in cage - Joseph or Joachim
2 Doves and model church - Withburga
Eagle - John the Evangelist
Partridge - Jerome
Swan and flowers - Hugh of Lincoln (Bishop)

Anchor - Clement or Nicholas (Bishop)
Anvil - Adrian or Eloy (Bishop)
Armour, in and trampling on Devil - Michael
Armour, in and on a white horse and spearing dragon - George
Arrow, piercing breast or hand - Giles or Egedius
Arrow piercing crown - Edmund
Arrows, pierced by, and bound to tree and young and naked - Sebastian
Axe - Matthias

Bag of Money - Matthew
3 Balls - Nicholas
Banner with red cross and surrounded by virgins - Ursula
Basket of fruit and flowers - Dorothea
Basket with loaves - Philip
Basket or Pitcher - Zita
Bedstead - Faith

Beehive - Ambrose, Bernard of Clairvaux or John Chrysostom
Beggar having his feet washed by Edith of Wilton
Beggar or Cripple receiving half of the cloak of Martin
Bell - Anthony
Boat - Jude
Bones - Ambrose
Book - many saints hold a Gospel
Book and Crook - Chad
Books - Ambrose or Boniface
Bottle - James the Great
Alabaster Box or Vase - Mary of Magdala (with long hair)
Breasts, on a plate - Agatha
Builder's Square - Thomas
Bundle of Rods - Faith

Candle, with devil blowing it out - Genevieve
Cauldron of oil - Vitus
Chains being held by Leonard (Deacon)
Child, crucified - William of Norwich
Child Jesus on shoulder and crossing river - Christopher
Child on arm - Anthony of Padua
2 Children being carried - Eustace
3 Children in tub - Nicholas
4 Children (sons) - Mary wife of Cleophas
Church, model of - Withburga with doves at her feet or Botolph
                   (Abbot) or other Founders
Cloth with face of Christ imprinted - Veronica
Comb, iron - Blaise (Bishop)
Cross, red on white - George
Cross, saltire - Andrew
Cross, inverted - Peter
T-Cross on shoulder - Anthony
T-Cross - Philip
True Cross - Helen

Demon at feet of man in white habit - Norbert
Devil with bellows - Genevieve
Devil being trampled on by man in armour - Michael

Eyes on a dish - Lucy

Feather - Barbara
Flame in hand or breast - Anthony of Padua
Floral emblems
   Crown of Roses - Cecilia
   Crown of Roses or holding Roses - Dorothy or Teresa
   Lily - Euphemia or Joseph or Dominic (black friar)
   Olive branch - Agnes
   Palm - Agnes or other martyr
   Tree, prostrate with foot of Boniface on it (Bishop)
   Tree - Etheldreda asleep under it

Gridiron - Laurence or Vincent

Halberd - Jude
Head, crowned and carried by Cuthbert (Bishop) or Denis (Bishop)
Head, man's under feet of Catherine of Alexandra

Head, being carried by herself before an altar - Winefred or Osyth
Heart, flaming or transfixed by sword - Augustine of Hippo
Hermit - Anthony
Hook, iron - Faith or Vincent
Horseshoe - Eloy

Idols, broken - Wilfrid, baptising pagans

Keys - Peter, or Zita or Martha with keys at girdle
Knife and skin over arm - Bartholomew

Loaves - Olaf or Zita
Loaves and fishes - disciples

Manacles - St Leobard holding them
Musical instruments - Cecilia

Pagans being baptised - Wilfrid
Pen, ink and scroll - Mark or Matthew or Bernard of Clairvaux and
                      others
Picture of Virgin Mary - Luke
Pincers - Agatha or Dunstan or Apollonia if holding tooth
Pot of Holy Water and Ladle - Martha

Saw - Simon
Scallop Shell - James the Great of Compostella
Scourge - Ambrose
Scyth and two calves - Walstan
Scyth and carrying head - Sidwell or Sativola
Shears - Agatha
Sieve, broken - Benedict
Staff - James the Great or James the Less or Bridget of Sweden
        (Abbess)
Stone striking head - Stephen (Deacon)
Surgical Instruments - Cosmos and Damian (always together, in red
                       robes)
Sword - Paul or Barbara
Sword through breast - Euphemia
Sword through neck - Lucy

Together - Cosmos and Damian or Raphael and Tobias carrying fish
Tower - Barbara

Weighing souls - Michael
Wheel - Catherine of Alexandria, with man's head under feet
Windlas - Erasmus, Bishop
Winged man - Matthew
Wounded forehead (red band) - Bridget of Sweden, Abbess
Wounded leg - Roch, also with angel, dog, staff and/or shell
Wounds of Christ (stigmata) - Francis of Assisi

ADRIAN   Anvil, lion
AGATHA   Dish containing her breasts, pincers or shears
AGNES   Olive branch, lamb, palm
AIDAN   Stag at his feet
ALBAN   Sword, fountain, sometimes his head in his hand, mace
ALPHEGE   Chasuble full of stones
AMBROSE   Beehive, books, two human bones, scourge
**ANDREW   Saltire Cross
ANTHONY   Hermit, a bell, a hog, a nearby fire, T-cross on shoulder
ANTONY of PADUA Franciscan habit, infant Jesus in arms, a flame
                 in his hand or on his breast, a kneeling mule
APOLLONIA   Pincers holding tooth
AUGUSTINE of CANTERBURY Archbishop
AUGUSTINE of HIPPO Bishop, books, sometimes a heart flaming or
                    transfixed by a sword
BARBARA   Patron of armourers, cup and wafer, tower, feather, sword,
              crown
**BARNABAS   Tudor roses on a shield or the Gospel
**BARTHOLOMEW Knife, his skin held over his arm
BENEDICT   Benedictine habit, broken cup, sprinkler, raven with a
              loaf in its beak, a broken sieve
BERNARD of CLAIRVAUX White habit, beehive, inkhorn, pen, three
                      mitres, sometimes a bound demon
BLAISE   Bishop, patron of woolcombers, iron comb
BONIFACE   Archbishop, Benedictine, book transfixed by a sword or
              stained with blood, foot on prostrate tree
BOTOLPH   Abbot
BRIDGET of SWEDEN Crozier, staff, red band across forehead
CATHERINE of ALEXANDRIA Wheel, head of man under her feet
CECILIA   Crown of roses, musical instruments
CHAD   Book and Crook - see also p.47
CHRISTOPHER   Carrying infant Jesus across river
CLARA   Nun, cross, lily, pyx
CLEMENT   Pope or Bishop's robes, anchor
CONSTANTINE   Labarum
COSMAS and DAMIAN always together, surgical instruments, red robes
CUTHBERT   Bishop, an otter by his side, holds St Oswald's crowned
              head
DAVID of WALES Bishop, Bible, dove on shoulder
DENIS   Bishop, carries his own head
DOMINIC   Black and white habit and black and white dogs with
              torches in their mouths, star on forehead, lily
DOROTHY   Crown of roses or holding roses in her hand or basket of
              fruit and flowers
DUNSTAN   A gold covered cup on a blue field, or red hot pincers
EDITH of WILTON washing a beggar's feet
EDMUND   King and martyr, an arrow piercing his crown, a wolf
              nearby guarding his head - sometimes he carries an arrow
EDWARD   King, sceptre surmounted by a dove
ELOY, LO, or ELIGIUS Bishop, an anvil or horseshoe
ELIZABETH   Mother of John the Baptist, in scene of Salutation
ERASMUS   Bishop
ETHELDREDA   Nun's habit, crowned, building a church, or asleep under
              a tree

EUPHEMIA   Sword through her breast, lion, lily
EUSTACE   Stag with crucifix between horns, or carrying two
                children across river, or two children carried off
                by beasts
FAITH   Carries a bundle of rods, iron hook or bedstead
FRANCIS of ASSISI Birds, lamb, lily, stigmata
FRIEDESWEIDA   Crowned Abbess, holds Gospels
GENEVIEVE   Distaff, sheep, basket of loaves, lighted candle with a
                demon blowing it out with bellows, angel lighting it
GEORGE   Red cross on white ground on banner or breast, white
                horse, he spears a dragon
GILES or EGIDIUS Arrow piercing his breast or through his hand, a
                nearby hind pierced by an arrow
GREGORY   Pope, dove on shoulder or hovering overhead
HELEN   Empress, holds large cross (True Cross)
HUBERT   Bishop, stag with crucifix between horns
HUGH of LINCOLN Carthusian habit, swan, three flowers
IVES or YVO   Lawyer's robes, sometimes surrounded by widows and
                orphans
**JAMES the GREAT Scallop shell, staff, bottle
**JAMES the LESS Fuller's staff or club
JEROME   Cardinal in the desert or in his study, lion, partridge
JOACHIM   Father of Virgin Mary, meeting St Anna at the gate,
                carries basket with two doves
JOHN the Baptist Lamb, tall staff with cross-piece, hairy coat
JOHN CHRYSOSTOM Beehive, chalice, gospels
JOHN de MATHA   White habit with blue and red cross on breast,
                fetters, angels leading captives
**JOHN the EVANGELIST Eagle, cup with serpent
JOSEPH   Lily
**JUDE   Halberd or boat
JULIANA   Holds dragon or devil by a chain, hangs by her hair
JULIAN   see p.47 (a blue cross-crosslet saltirewise on a silver
                field)
LAURENCE   Gridiron
LEONARD   Deacon or Abbot, holds chains or manicles
LOUIS IX   Crown of thorns, royal robes or Franciscan habit
LUCY   Eyes in a dish, sword, wound in neck, lamp
**LUKE the EVANGELIST Ox, a picture of the Virgin Mary
MARGARET of ANTIOCH A dragon or cross
**MARK the EVANGELIST Lion, pen, ink, scroll
MARTHA   Keys at girdle, pot of holy water, ladle, dragon bound
                at feet
MARTIN   Beggar or cripple at his feet receiving half his cloak
MARY, wife of Cleophas and mother of James, John, Simeon and Joseph,
                shown with her four sons and bearing their emblems
MARY MAGDALENE Box or vase of alabaster, long hair
**MATTHEW the EVANGELIST Winged man, ink, scroll, pen, bag of
                money, knife or dagger
**MATTHIAS   An axe
NICHOLAS   Bishop, ship, anchor, three balls, three children in tub
NORBERT   White habit over black, demon bound at feet, cup with
                spider over it
OLAF   Loaves

OSWALD   King, large cross
OSYTH or SYTHA Queen, Abbess, carries her head
**PAUL   Sword
**PETER   Keys, fish, inverted cross
PETER the Martyr Dominican with wound in head
**PHILIP   Cross, sometimes T-shaped, basket with loaves
RADEGUNDA   Crowned abbess, a captive kneeling at her feet, broken
              fetters in her hand
ROCH   Points to a wound in his leg, staff, shell, dog by his
              side, angel
SEBASTIAN   Bound to a tree or column and pierced by arrows
SIDWELL or SATIVOLA Scyth and well, carries her head
**SIMON   Fishes, saw
STEPHEN   Deacon, a stone striking his head
SWITHIN   Bishop of Winchester
TERESA of AVILA Brown habit, roses
**THOMAS   Builder's square
THOMAS AQUINAS Dominican, star on breast
THOMAS à BECKET Archbishop, Benedictine, wound in his head
URSULA   Banner with a red cross, sometimes surrounded by virgins
VERONICA   Holding a cloth on which is the face of Christ
VINCENT   Deacon, raven and lion, iron hook
VITUS   Cauldron of oil, boy with palm, cock, lion or wolf
WALSTAN   King holding a scythe, two calves
WILFRID   Baptising pagans, broken idols around
WILLIAM of NORWICH A child being crucified
WINEFRED   Carrying her head before an altar
WITHBURGA   Two doves at her feet, a church in her hand
WULFSTAN, WULSTAN or WOLSTAN Bishop, fixing his crozier in St
                              Edward's tomb, devil behind him with a
                              book - giving sight to a blind man
ZITA, CITHA or SITHA Housekeeper with keys, loaves or rosary, bag,
                      pitcher or basket

**APOSTLES - always twelve, but not always the same ones, sometimes
             Jude, Simon and Matthias are omitted

   AND

   EVANGELISTS - John (eagle)
                 Luke (winged ox)
                 Mark (winged lion)
                 Matthew (winged man)

BENEDICTINE (habit all black) Benedict or Boniface or Thomas à
             Becket.

CARMELITE   (since 1287 a white cloak over brown habit) John de
             Matha, with blue and red cross on breast, fetters, or
             with angel and leading captives.

CARTHUSIAN   (white serge) Hugh of Lincoln, with swan and three
             flowers.

CISTERCIAN   (white or grey) Bernard of Clairvaux, with three crowns.

DOMINICAN   (white tunic, black cloak with hood) Dominic, with star
             on forehead and two dogs with torches in their mouths.
             Peter the martyr, with wound in head.
             Thomas Aquinas, with chalice and star on breast.

FRANCISCAN   (brown, sometimes grey) Francis of Assisi, with
             animals. Anthony of Padua, with infant Jesus on arm.
             Louis IX, with crown of thorns.

HAIRY COAT   John the Baptist, with staff and cross-piece and lamb.

Knights Templar (not saints) wear a white wool habit with red cross.
Knights of St John of Jerusalem wear a long wide black tunic with
             white cross on breast and the higher ranks a red
             surcoat with white cross.

MARTYRS   usually hold a palm.
HERMITS   usually hold a T shaped staff and a rosary.
PILGRIMS wear a hat with a shell and carry a staff and wallet.
FOUNDERS usually hold models of churches or monasteries.
BISHOPS and ABBOTS hold a crozier or pastoral staff.
POPES   wear a triple tiara, cope and pallium, and hold a triple
          cross.

TEXTS will be found in the Bible - a Commentary on the Bible is
             sometimes useful.
             St Matthew's Gospel is a rich source and includes in
             chapters V-VII the Beatitudes.
             The Gifts of the Holy Spirit are in the Book of Isaiah XI.
             The Fruits of the Spirit will be found in Paul's letter to
             the Galatians V.

Some ROYALS

King, with sceptre surmounted by dove, sometimes with a wolf and
     an arrow - EDMUND.
King, holding large cross - OSWALD.
Queen, holding large cross - HELEN.
Emperor, holding labarum - CONSTANTINE.
King, in royal robes or Franciscan habit, crowned with thorns -
     LOUIS IX.
Queen, in habit of an Abbess - FRIEDESWEIDE.

Cardinal, in study or desert - Jerome.
Archbishop - Boniface or Augustine of Canterbury or Thomas à Becket.

ANGELIC ORDERS

Seraphim and Cherubim usually have six wings which may be strewn
with eyes.
Thrones are represented as scarlet wheels with wings and sometimes
with eyes.
The above three Orders are sometimes depicted as warriors or judges.

ARCHANGELS: Gabriel (Annunciation), Michael (Resurrection and
                weighing the souls of departed), Raphael (with Tobias
                and fish), Uriel.

ANGELS: usually have a pair of wings and are nimbed: may hold
                scrolls, instruments of the Passion or musical
                instruments.

PROPHETS: Isaiah, Jeremiah, Ezekiel, Daniel,
                Hosea, Joel, Amos, Obadiah, Jonah, Micah, Nahum,
                Habakkuk, Zephaniah, Haggai, Zechariah, Malachi.

TYPES and ANTITYPES are often portrayed in Christian decoration:
                incidents in the Old Testament (types) foreshadow
                corresponding incidents in the New Testament (anti-
                types), for example Jonah's escape, after three days,
                from the whale is a type of the Resurrection when
                Christ's body remained for that time in the tomb.
                This is well described in 'An Illustrated Guide to the
                Windows of King's College Chapel Cambridge' by Kenneth
                Harrison (1965). Many of the windows in the chapel
                adhere to the scheme of type and antitype. The booklet
                might also serve as a reminder of Biblical stories.

Aaron	ROD and SERPENT
Abel	CROOK and LAMB
Abraham	KNIFE and SHIELD
Amos	CROOK
Cain	PLOUGH
Daniel	RAM with four horns
David	HARP and LION
Deborah	CROWN
Elijah	FIERY CHARIOT
Esau	BOW and ARROWS
Ezekiel	CLOSED GATE
Gideon	TORCH conceiled in PITCHER
Hosea	CAST-OFF MANTLE
Isaiah	SAW
Isaac	CROSS formed of bundles of wood
Jacob and family	SUN, MOON and 12 STARS
Jeremiah	LARGE STONE
Jonah	WHALE
Joseph	COAT of many COLOURS
Joshua	TRUMPET and SWORD
Melchisedek	LOAF of BREAD and CHALICE
Micah	TEMPLE on a MOUNTAIN
Moses	BASKET of BULRUSHES, BURNING BUSH, HORNS, TABLETS
Nahum	FEET appearing from a cloud above a mountain
Noah	ARK or OAR
Ruth	WHISP of WHEAT
Samson	JAWBONE of Ass and PILLARS
Seth	THREAD wound three times around THUMB
Solomon	MODEL of TEMPLE
Zephaniah	SWORD hanging over Jerusalem

A FLAMING SWORD represents Adam's expulsion, and a SPADE his future
way of life; that of Eve is represented by a DISTAFF.
A SERPENT represents Satan and when it is coiled around the world it
represents the sinful nature of mankind.
An APPLE represents the Fall of Man.
A DRAGON may represent Satan, sin or pestilence. When underfoot it
signifies victory over evil.
A DOVE with an Olive Sprig denotes peace and forgiveness.
A LASH and BRICKS represent Israel's captivity.
A CLUSTER of GRAPES represents Entry into Canaan.
ALTAR of SACRIFICE and ALTAR of BURNT OFFERING - Old Testament
worship.
ARK of the COVENANT is the symbol of the Presence of God.
LAMB (Paschal Lamb) represents Passover Festival.
DOORPOSTS and LINTEL symbol of God's protection and Passover.
SCROLL and SHEAF of WHEAT represent Pentecost.
SCROLL (by itself) represents the Torah or Five Books of Moses.
YOUNG BULLOCK and CENSER symbolize Day of Atonement.
SEVEN-BRANCH CANDLESTICK known as the Menorah represents Old
Testament worship.

Prophecy of Simeon. Appearance of Gabriel to aged Zacharius. Annunciation of Gabriel to VM. Visitation of VM to cousin Elizabeth. Joachim and Anna, parents of VM. Anna teaching VM to read.

Nativity. Adoration of Shepherds and of the Magi (Caspar usually old with long beard, Melchior middle-aged with short beard, Balthasar, the youngest, beardless and sometimes a negro). Circumcision (baby). Presentation in Temple (child). Massacre of Innocents. Flight into Egypt. Guide leads to town of Sotinen. Casting out of Moneylenders and Teaching in Temple. Baptism by John.

All the Parables and Miracles including Good Samaritan with Gentile and Pharisee, Mary Magdalene washing Christ's feet, Pearl of Great Price, Raising of Lazarus, Raising of Jarus's daughter, Sower of seeds, Wedding at Cana, Wise and Foolish Virgins, Prodigal Son, Talents, Feeding of 4,000 with 7 loaves and 3 fishes, Feeding of 5,000 with 5 loaves and 2 fishes, Miraculous draught of fishes.

Entry into Jerusalem. Agony in the Garden. Last Supper. Peter hears cock crowing. Peter strikes off ear of Melchius. Trial before Pilate and Caiaphas. Scourging at pillar. Crowning with thorns. *Stations of the Cross. Crucifixion (VM and Longinius, the soldier with lance on Christ's right, John and Stephaton with reed and sponge on His left).

Deposition (taking down from cross). Pietà (Virgin Mary holding body and showing wounds). Joseph of Arimathea pulling out nails and taking body for burial. Three Marys at tomb with angel and soldier at Resurrection. 'Noli me tangere' (Mary Magdalene encountering Christ at tomb). Incredulity of Thomas.

Christ's appearance to apostles in closed room. Appearance to James the great and Cleopas on road to Emmaus. Supper (with two) in Emmaus, which should not be confused with the appearance of the Trinity to Abraham (Genesis XVIII) when the three figures have rayed nimbi.

Ascension. Descent of Holy Ghost to Apostles. Assumption. Coronation of Virgin Mary and the Glory of all the saints. Christ's descent into Limbo. The Last Judgment (Doom).

*STATIONS OF THE CROSS
1. Jesus condemned to death. 2. Jesus receives the cross. 3. Jesus falls for the first time under the cross. 4. Jesus meets his mother. 5. Simon of Cyrene bears the cross. 6. Veronica wipes the face of Jesus. 7. Jesus falls the second time. 8. Jesus meets the women of Jerusalem. 9. Jesus falls the third time. 10. Jesus is stripped of his garments. 11. Jesus is nailed to the cross. 12. Jesus dies on the cross. 13. Jesus is taken down from the cross. 14. The body of Jesus is laid in the sepulchre.

WORDS from the Cross
Luke XXIII 34, Luke XXIII 43, John XIX 26, Matthew XXVII 46, John XIX 28, John XIX 30, Luke XXIII 46.

Hand of God
Latin form

Power
or
Blessing

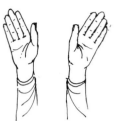

Early attitude of
prayer pre-9th century

as above

as above
Greek form

Blessing   Judgment
(see 'Doom' p.186)

as above

Hand of God
with Souls
of Righteous

Supplication

Condemnation

Hand of God
Judgment

Speech

Argument

Symbols of The Holy Trinity

Trefoil

Bezel
or
Interlocking
Triangles

Triquetra

Circle
within
Triangle

Interwoven
Circles

Triquetra
and
Circle

The Holy Trinity

Trinity Star
or
Star of David

Equilateral
Triangle

The
Three
Fishes

The Three Hares

Triangle
in Circle

Shield with
Doctrine of the
Blessed Trinity

Seven Lamps or Seven Flames   Seven Doves

The Gifts of the Holy Spirit
Wisdom   Ghostly Strength
Understanding   Knowledge
Counsel   True Godliness
Holy Fear

The Dove
(Holy Spirit)

Agnus Dei with the
Banner of Victory

Agnus Dei and the
Book of Seven Seals

Paschal Lamb (Old Testament)

The letters spell
'Fish' in Greek
and stand for
'Jesus Christ Son
of God, Saviour'

The Pelican in her Piety

EMBLEMS
of
The Virgin Mary

Mater Dei

Fleur-de-Lys

Lily

Crescent
Moon

Mystic Rose

Snowdrop

Winged Heart

Pierced Heart

EMBLEMS
of
The Evangelists

St Matthew

St Mark

St Luke

St John

STARS

Seven Gifts of the Spirit

Nine Fruits of the Spirit

Twelve Tribes of Israel

Regeneration

Creator's

Epiphany

SACRED MONOGRAMS
CHI RHO
the first two
letters of
XPICTOC (Christ)

IHC or IHS
the first letters
of IHCOYC (Jesus)

Jesus Christ Victor

NIKA (Victor)

N can signify NIKA or
NOSTRA (our)

CHI RHO with ALPHA
and OMEGA in a Circle
(symbol of Christ
within symbol for
eternity)

ALPHA-MU-OMEGA
(yesterday, today
and forever)

The CORNERSTONE

ALPHA and OMEGA
(the first and last
letters of the
Greek alphabet -
Beginning and End
of all things)

SYMBOLS OF THE PASSION

Crown of Thorns

Sponge on Reed

Nails

Thirty Pieces
of Silver

Scourges

Hammer and Pincers

Seamless Robe

The Cock
that crowed

Cross with Sheet

Pillar and Cords

The Title

Jug of Vinegar

Lantern

The Fist
that buffeted Him

Five Wounds

Agony in Gethsemane

Ladder

Sword and Staff

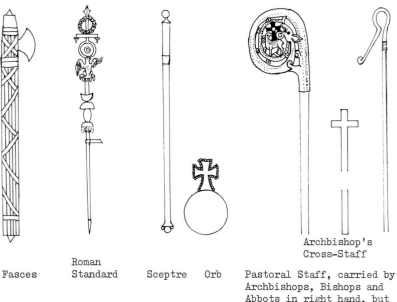

Archbishop's
Cross-Staff

Fasces   Roman   Sceptre   Orb   Pastoral Staff, carried by
             Standard   Archbishops, Bishops and
                                             Abbots in right hand, but
                                                   held in left hand
                                                   during benediction.

Three-rayed NIMBUS reserved for persons   Nimbus
of the Trinity.   as worn by others, unless
                                            at the time of represent-
                                            ation the person is
                                            living, when it is
                                            SQUARE.

BIBLIOGRAPHY

CHILD, H. and COLLES, D. (1971), 'Christian Symbols Ancient and
Modern', Bell, London.
ELLWOOD POST, W. (1964), 'Saints, Signs and Symbols', SPCK, London.
ROUSE, C.E. (1968), 'Discovering Wall Paintings', Shire Publications,
Aylesbury.
WHITTEMORE, CARROLL E. (1959), 'Symbols of the Church', Hodder &
Stoughton, London.

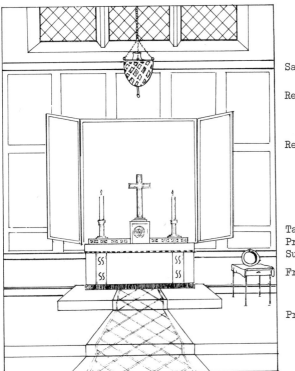

Sanctuary Lamp

Reredos
(if a curtain, it
is a Dossall)

Retable
(the one illus-
trated is a
triptych retable)

Tabernacle
Predella (the shelf)
Superfrontal

Frontal
(see also Laudian
and Antependium)

Predella (the step)

ALTAR	Sometimes a table, usually a purpose-built frame.
ANTEPENDIUM	A carved or painted panel serving as altar façade.
CREDENCE	The serving-table on the South side of the altar.
FRONTAL	Altar façade of textile.
SUPER FRONTAL	A band, usually fringed, sometimes contrasting, overlapping the top of the frontal.
LAUDIAN	A loose throw-over altar covering (see TEXTILES).
MENSA	Term usually reserved for a stone table-top, with or without five incised crosses.
PREDELLA (or gradin)	Shelf at rear of altar-top - also the term for the step on which the altar stands.
REREDOS	Screen covering the wall behind and above the altar: when made of wood it is sometimes called a RETABLUM.
RETABLE	Altar-piece behind, but attached to, or standing on the predella.
	Also the name of a shelf between altar and East wall, but not to be confused with the predella.
	Pugin used the term 'super altar' for the 20th century use of RETABLE, but here the definition in the 'Oxford Dictionary' is given.
TABERNACLE	Receptable for the pyx - sometimes hangs from the ceiling and is covered by a veil.

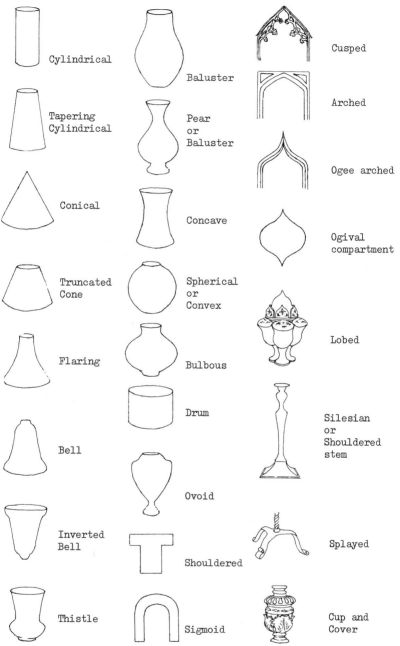

Cylindrical

Tapering
Cylindrical

Conical

Truncated
Cone

Flaring

Bell

Inverted
Bell

Thistle

Baluster

Pear
or
Baluster

Concave

Spherical
or
Convex

Bulbous

Drum

Ovoid

Shouldered

Sigmoid

Cusped

Arched

Ogee arched

Ogival
compartment

Lobed

Silesian
or
Shouldered
stem

Splayed

Cup and
Cover

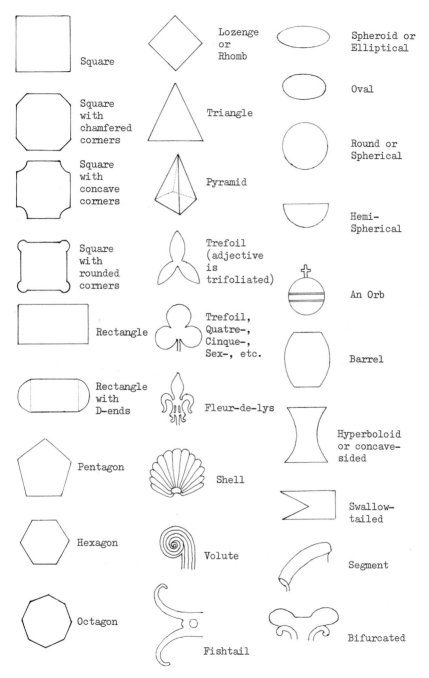

Square

Square with chamfered corners

Square with concave corners

Square with rounded corners

Rectangle

Rectangle with D-ends

Pentagon

Hexagon

Octagon

Lozenge or Rhomb

Triangle

Pyramid

Trefoil (adjective is trifoliated)

Trefoil, Quatre-, Cinque-, Sex-, etc.

Fleur-de-lys

Shell

Volute

Fishtail

Spheroid or Elliptical

Oval

Round or Spherical

Hemi-Spherical

An Orb

Barrel

Hyperboloid or concave-sided

Swallow-tailed

Segment

Bifurcated

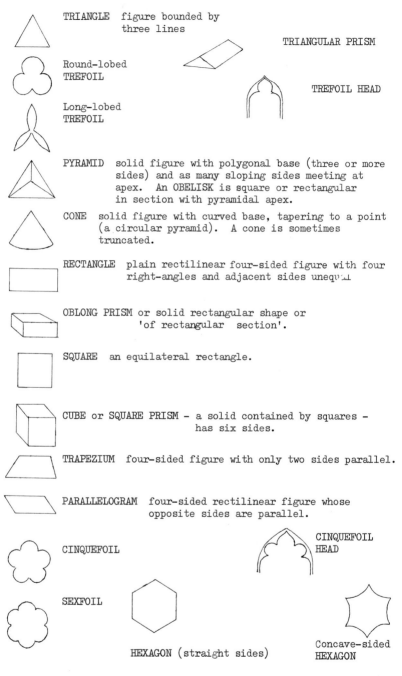

TRIANGLE   figure bounded by
           three lines

TRIANGULAR PRISM

Round-lobed
TREFOIL

TREFOIL HEAD

Long-lobed
TREFOIL

PYRAMID   solid figure with polygonal base (three or more
          sides) and as many sloping sides meeting at
          apex. An OBELISK is square or rectangular
          in section with pyramidal apex.

CONE   solid figure with curved base, tapering to a point
       (a circular pyramid). A cone is sometimes
       truncated.

RECTANGLE   plain rectilinear four-sided figure with four
            right-angles and adjacent sides unequal.

OBLONG PRISM or solid rectangular shape or
             'of rectangular section'.

SQUARE   an equilateral rectangle.

CUBE or SQUARE PRISM - a solid contained by squares -
                      has six sides.

TRAPEZIUM   four-sided figure with only two sides parallel.

PARALLELOGRAM   four-sided rectilinear figure whose
                opposite sides are parallel.

CINQUEFOIL

CINQUEFOIL
HEAD

SEXFOIL

HEXAGON (straight sides)

Concave-sided
HEXAGON

BALUSTER
also called
PEAR or TULIP

Baluster

Squat Baluster

(Pewter vessels
are called bulbous
or bellied)

Bombé

CYLINDRICAL

Tapering
Cylindrical

Tall
Cylindrical

Tall Tapering
Cylindrical

BARREL

BARREL

BOAT

DRUM

HELMET

URN or VASE
or OVOID

Hexagonal
stepped
stand or
socle

Plate-shaped

Dish-shaped or
Basin-shaped

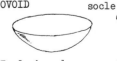

Bowl-shaped or
Saucer-shaped if
shallower

Cup-
shaped

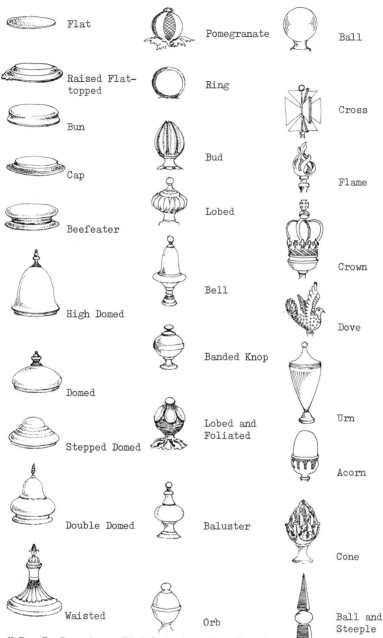

Flat

Raised Flat-
topped

Bun

Cap

Beefeater

High Domed

Domed

Stepped Domed

Double Domed

Waisted

Pomegranate

Ring

Bud

Lobed

Bell

Banded Knop

Lobed and
Foliated

Baluster

Orb

Ball

Cross

Flame

Crown

Dove

Urn

Acorn

Cone

Ball and
Steeple

N.B. In Ceramics a Finial is termed a 'Knop'.

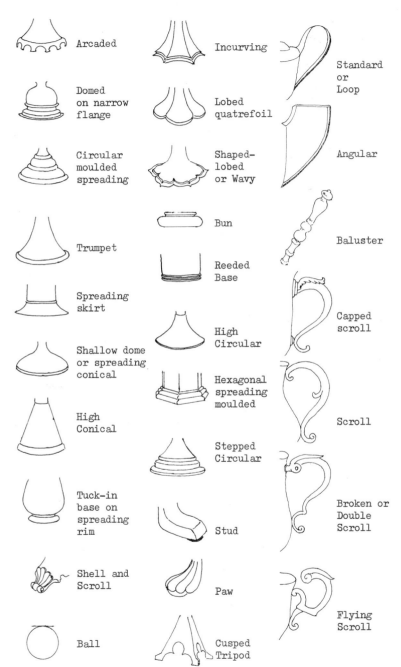

Arcaded

Domed
on narrow
flange

Circular
moulded
spreading

Trumpet

Spreading
skirt

Shallow dome
or spreading
conical

High
Conical

Tuck-in
base on
spreading
rim

Shell and
Scroll

Ball

Incurving

Lobed
quatrefoil

Shaped-
lobed
or Wavy

Bun

Reeded
Base

High
Circular

Hexagonal
spreading
moulded

Stepped
Circular

Stud

Paw

Cusped
Tripod

Standard
or
Loop

Angular

Baluster

Capped
scroll

Scroll

Broken or
Double
Scroll

Flying
Scroll

Spherical

Compressed
or Proper

Lobed

Wrythen or
Spiralling

Hexagonal

Lobed
Gothic

Wrythen or
Spiralling
Gothic

Compressed
and
Annulated

Bladed -
sometimes called a
'flange'

Compressed
knot above
a flange

Lobed
flange

Swelling

Cup and
Cover or
Melon

Shouldered

Mushroom

Dumb-bell

Cushioned

Cone

Acorn

Multi-
knopped

As for woodwork, architectural terminology is used for stonework and the names of the techniques are similar.

No recorder should be without the 'Illustrated Glossary of Architecture' by Harris and Lever mentioned in the bibliography, in which every term is defined and illustrated with a photograph and vaulting is fully described.

In this section the following have not been illustrated as the same terminology will be found in the sample descriptions in the woodwork section:

Pulpit

Screen (pulpitum, reredos, retable, parclose)

Feretory (the name also applies to a room or chapel in which relicts are kept)

A FEW TERMS

Mouldings	– projecting or recessed ornamental bands, see p.237.
Chamfer	– the surface formed when an angle is cut away obliquely: it may be moulded, concave (hollow), sunk or stopped.
Reveal	– the inside surface of door or window cut at right angles.
Splay	– the same cut diagonally.
Tabernaclework	– elaborate carved work on canopies over niches, stalls, etc.

14th century
EASTER SEPULCHRE

Canopied recess of
three bays with
crocketed, pinnacled
and cusped ogee
arches, above a table-
top tomb with four
panels of similar blind
arched decoration.

Adjacent on the W side
is a floor-level similar
recess.
(sample description)

EASTER SEPULCHRE canopied recess in North Chancel wall, with table
top tomb used to contain the Sacrament or effigy of Christ at
Easter. A few exquisite examples in the UK are of wood. Describe
as for a tomb in a canopied recess.

PISCINA in S wall of
chancel: the above
example has a
CREDENCE shelf
A similar recess adjacent
to a door is usually a STOUP

AUMBRY
a cupboard in
N wall of
chancel

BREAD OVEN

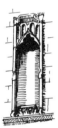

Empty NICHE

SQUINT
or HAGIOSCOPE
with view of altar

BANNER CUPBOARD

14th century SEDILIA
of clunch, in range
with the Piscina

Sub-cusped cinquefoiled
ogee heads which are
crocketed and finialed.

Detached cylindrical
shafts, with moulded
capitals and bases,
separate the three
stepped seats and
piscina.
(sample description)

A SEDILIA is a set of stone seats, usually canopied and
decorated, in the South wall of the chancel. Sometimes
a windowsill is utilised as such.

A PISCINA is
smaller, higher and
usually has a drain

CREDENCE
usually a table, but
sometimes a stone shelf

13th century Sedilia

Stone brackets for statuettes,
the one on the right with
moulded 13th century
dog-tooth ornament

CORBEL

Saxon MENSA (stone altar)

originally with five
Consecration Crosses
on the top.
20th century tapering pillar
supports.
(sample description)

Saxon Drum Font
with lead-lined bowl decorated with
crudely carved Latin crosses within
arcading. Two bands of cable moulding
above the stepped base.

Norman pedestal font with square bowl,
following the form of a capital, with
roundels containing moulded patterns
alternating with large heads at the
corners. Short octagonal stem
springing from the drum pedestal.

Remains of iron staple on rim for
locking flat cover.

Norman font with cup bowl,
elaborately carved with chevron around
the rim and patterns and stiff leaf on
the body: it is supported on a massive
central cylindrical stem.
Four angle-shafts, rising from a square
plinth, outside the bowl, support
projecting masks against the sides of
the top of the bowl.

Mediaeval stone Font and stone CANOPY

The canopy, supported on six shafts
standing on an hexagonal plinth, has
a high dome, with decorated ribs, and
encircled by reeded panelling.

The font has an hexagonal
bowl and stem and stands on a stepped
hexagonal base in the centre of the
plinth.

Caen stone c.1873.

Octagonal bowl with carved representations of the four
Evangelists and their symbols, alternating with kneeling angels,
each under a crocketed ogee canopy, in the panels.

Bosses of demi-angels at the points of intersection beneath the
pinnacled buttresses which separate the panels.

Octagonal stem ornamented with shields bearing symbols of the
Passion on the panels between engaged shafts. Oakleaf motifs
in a coved section beneath the bowl. The moulded bases of the
shafts stand on a stepped octagonal plinth.

A large stepped and moulded cruciform plinth of Mansfield stone
supports the font.

BIBLIOGRAPHY

CHILD, M. (1976), 'Discovering Church Architecture', Shire
Publications, Aylesbury (for beginners).
HARRIES, J. (1972), 'Discovering Churches', Shire Publications,
Aylesbury.
HARRIS, J. and LEVER, J. (1966), 'Illustrated Glossary of
Architecture 850-1830', Faber & Faber, London.
JONES, L.E. (1965), 'The Observer's Book of Old English Churches',
Warne, London.
PEVSNER, N., Buildings of England Series, Penguin, Harmondsworth.
THE ROYAL COMMISSION ON HISTORICAL MONUMENTS.

A fine carpet is judged by the quality of the wool, the tightness of the weave (in general the more knots per square inch the better and there can be several hundred), the shape and sheen and the clarity of the design and its beauty.

The first step should be to learn to distinguish between pile, flat-woven and embroidered carpets: then to recognise the seven main oriental groups, before attempting to identify the individual types within the groups. A reliable dealer will explain the fundamental points, there are many books on the subject and visits to museums to learn to know the best - all will help.

Anything over a hundred years old is 'antique', over sixty years old is 'semi-antique' and from twenty-five is 'old'.

Persian carpets have been copied since the 15th century by Spain, Poland (notable for European coats of arms), France (with the appearance of tapestry) and England, where they were copied in tent and cross stitch in the 16th and 17th centuries.

PERSIAN	Naturalistic splendour of decoration, repetitive all-over designs; central medallion, sometimes lobed or hung with festoons, decorated with pendants, lanterns and rectangular inscriptions; central motif often repeated at four corners. Gardens, hunting scenes and narratives, including Biblical, are typical. Sehna and Ghiordes knot.
TURKISH	Brilliant colours - seldom large - borders with seven ribbons decorated with flowers - mostly geometric patterns and representations of oriental mosque arch. No picture narratives and very little green colouring.
CAUCASIAN	Owing to invasions a great variety of styles - squared and positive geometric designs giving impression of mosaic enclosed in differently coloured bands arranged diagonally - dragons - soft rose relieved by dark blue or black. Ghiordes knot.
TURKOMAN	Basic colour a deep glowing red (a secret) - geometric patterns with wavy brown outlines - repetitive octagons and hexagons divided in various ways, sometimes cross-wise into four parts arranged in parallel and perpendicular rows, known as 'guls' (flowers) or 'elephant's foot'.
CHINESE	Much yellow - chief motifs dragon, phoenix, lion, bat, cloud, swastika, pomegranate. Modern ones often made in Japan.
INDIAN	Designs in French, Persian and Chinese style but usually in light pastel colours and made of cotton.
AFGHANISTAN	Wine-red field - large octagons.

Sehna Knot

pile thread twisted
round one warp.

Ghiordes Knot

Kelim
or Tapestry Weaving

usually the threads
are incorporated in
the weaving so that
the rug can be used
on either side.

Some usual types of PERSIAN

HAMADAN   dark geometric medallions standing out against background
of natural camelhair - tortoise motif - heavy - single
knotting different from others.

ISFAHAN   repeated representation of a hand grasping a phoenix -
finely woven - bright ground - symmetrical design - round
medallion with eight or sixteen points.

KASHAN   little flowers filling both the centre and the rich
borders - wool soft and silky - no symbols - bouquets
resembling peacock feathers - very valuable.

HERAT   closed rosettes in elongated leaves or ribbon-pattern
scroll or diamond - rosette with eight points - backgrounds dark blue or purple-red - main colour of border
green - very rich wool - rectangular shape - Ghiordes or
Sehna knot.

TABRIZ   large central medallion on plain background, repeated
and quartered at corners - four seasons pattern - hunting
scenes - Ghiordes or Sehna knot.

FERAGHAN   rusty background - palmettes and vegetation - Herati
pattern - not thick - green borders valuable.

HERIZ   geometric patterns well spaced on light backgrounds.

BIBLIOGRAPHY

CAMPANA, M. (1966), 'Oriental Carpets', Hamlyn, London.
***FOKKER, NICOLAS (1973), 'Persian and Other Oriental Carpets for
Today', Allen & Unwin, London (recommended).
TURKHAN, KUDRET H. (1968), 'Islamic Rugs', Arthur Barker, London.
WILSON, P. (1966), 'Antiques International', Hamlyn, London.

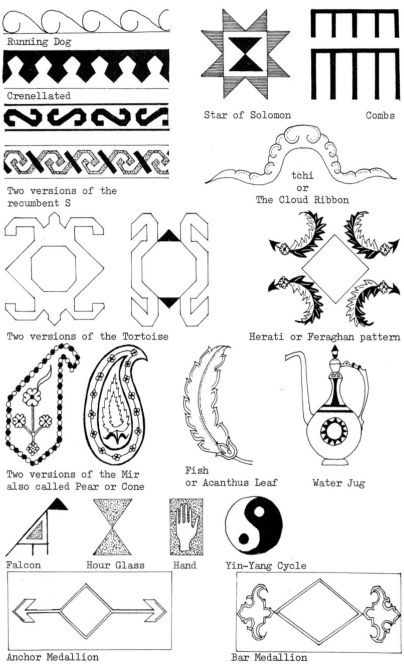

Running Dog

Crenellated

Two versions of the
recumbent S

Star of Solomon

Combs

tchi
or
The Cloud Ribbon

Two versions of the Tortoise

Herati or Feraghan pattern

Two versions of the Mir
also called Pear or Cone

Fish
or Acanthus Leaf

Water Jug

Falcon

Hour Glass

Hand

Yin-Yang Cycle

Anchor Medallion

Bar Medallion

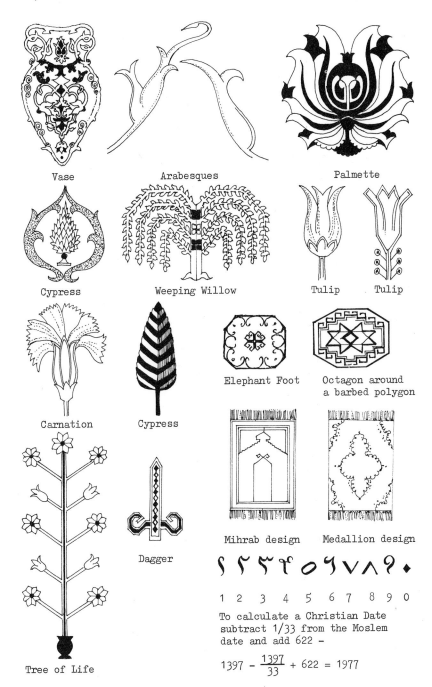

Vase

Arabesques

Palmette

Cypress

Weeping Willow

Tulip

Tulip

Carnation

Cypress

Elephant Foot

Octagon around
a barbed polygon

Tree of Life

Dagger

Mihrab design

Medallion design

ٮ ٮ ٮ ٮ ٠ ٮ ٧ ٨ ٩ ٠

1 2 3 4 5 6 7 8 9 0

To calculate a Christian Date
subtract 1/33 from the Moslem
date and add 622 –

$$1397 - \frac{1397}{33} + 622 = 1977$$

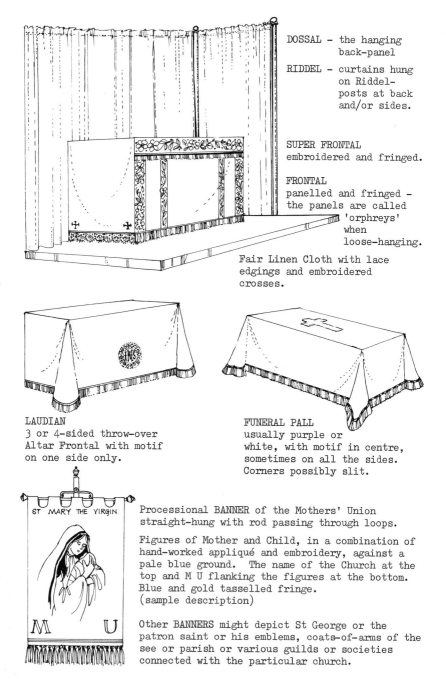

DOSSAL - the hanging back-panel

RIDDEL - curtains hung on Riddel-posts at back and/or sides.

SUPER FRONTAL
embroidered and fringed.

FRONTAL
panelled and fringed - the panels are called 'orphreys' when loose-hanging.

Fair Linen Cloth with lace edgings and embroidered crosses.

LAUDIAN
3 or 4-sided throw-over Altar Frontal with motif on one side only.

FUNERAL PALL
usually purple or white, with motif in centre, sometimes on all the sides. Corners possibly slit.

ST MARY THE VIRGIN

M   U

Processional BANNER of the Mothers' Union straight-hung with rod passing through loops.

Figures of Mother and Child, in a combination of hand-worked appliqué and embroidery, against a pale blue ground. The name of the Church at the top and M U flanking the figures at the bottom. Blue and gold tasselled fringe.
(sample description)

Other BANNERS might depict St George or the patron saint or his emblems, coats-of-arms of the see or parish or various guilds or societies connected with the particular church.

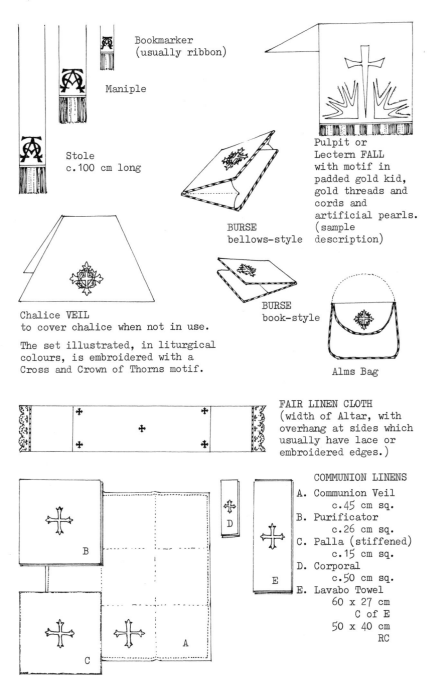

Bookmarker (usually ribbon)

Maniple

Stole
c.100 cm long

Pulpit or Lectern FALL with motif in padded gold kid, gold threads and cords and artificial pearls. (sample description)

BURSE bellows-style

Chalice VEIL
to cover chalice when not in use.

The set illustrated, in liturgical colours, is embroidered with a Cross and Crown of Thorns motif.

BURSE book-style

Alms Bag

FAIR LINEN CLOTH
(width of Altar, with overhang at sides which usually have lace or embroidered edges.)

COMMUNION LINENS
A. Communion Veil
      c.45 cm sq.
B. Purificator
      c.26 cm sq.
C. Palla (stiffened)
      c.15 cm sq.
D. Corporal
      c.50 cm sq.
E. Lavabo Towel
      60 x 27 cm
                  C of E
      50 x 40 cm
                  RC

CIBORIUM or PYX VEIL

White circular veil, with hole in centre, under which the Sacrament is reserved in the Tabernacle.

MONSTRANCE VEIL

Strip of white silk, without lining, with plain hemmed edges, nearly twice the height of the Monstrance.

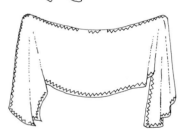

HUMERAL or OFFERTORY VEIL
c.270 cm x 60 cm

White linen shoulder scarf, usually unlined, worn by the priest when in procession or when moving the Sacrament from the Tabernacle.

TABERNACLE VEILS
in liturgical colours

Divided in the centre and with a hole in middle for a finial to protrude.

Other VEILS or CLOTHS are

Aumbry veil, sometimes embroidered, covering the Aumbry Door.
Communion Cloth, a small white linen napkin to catch crumbs.
Houseling Cloth, white linen, the length of the Altar Rails.

Pair of pale blue velvet
WEDDING KNEELERS
on each a white silk satin-stitch embroidered dove
picked out in black tent stitch.

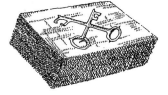

HASSOCK or KNEELER
with crossed keys embroidered in gold
silk petit-point against a shaded grey
wool gros-point field. Side edges
covered completely with red wool
cross-stitch.

Altar rail KNEELING PAD or BENCH RUNNER with bold Fish design and
water effect in gold and silver Kid Leathers, Cords and Metallic
threads. Emerald green velveteen sides.

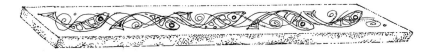

Red velvet altar
CUSHION
with corded edges
and long tassels
attached to the
corners by basket-
stitch.

Similar cushions are to be found
on the Credence, Pulpit and in
the Sanctuary Chair.

As well as DOSSALS and RIDDELS,
CURTAINS, often of beautiful materials, may be found over doors
and behind openwork screens.

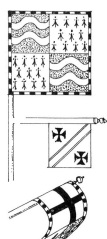

BANNER
square or rectangular - bearing the owner's
arms over the whole surface.
What is generally known as 'The Royal Standard'
is correctly 'The Sovereign's BANNER'.

A knight's banner should be approx. 90 cm sq.,
a prince's or a duke's approx. 123 cm sq. and
the sovereign's approx. 150 cm sq. - unless
they are rectangular.

BANNER ROLL
a small square containing a single escutcheon.

STANDARD
either a long tapering flag,
split at the end - bearing the
owners, devices, motto - but
never the arms or achievement -
or an emblem on a staff.

PENNON or GONFANNON
small pointed flag with two or more
streamers, borne at the lance-head:
the Gonfannon is fixed in a frame to
turn like a ship's vane.

VEXILLUM
a pennon attached to a staff.

UNION JACK or the UNION BANNER - the
National Ensign of the United Kingdom,
combining the National Banners of
England, Scotland and Ireland, which
may be flown on land by any British
subject.

An Infantry Regimental flag is called 'Colour'
when single, and 'Colours' when a pair.

A Cavalry Regimental flag, square or
rectangular, is called a 'Standard'.

A Processional Banner

Basically there are two different kinds:
      NEEDLEPOINT and PILLOW LACE
and both can be reproduced by machine since the late 18th century.

NEEDLEPOINT, developed from drawn-thread work, is made with a single
thread and needle, using embroidery stitches, dominated by
buttonhole stitch.

Ecclesiastical robes and textiles are often adorned by 'rose-
point', one of the many types of needlepoint, which consists of
patterns worked in relief like sculptured work, forming strong and
solid flowers and scrolls held in position by brides enriched with
picots.

PILLOW LACE, developed from knotted fringes and network, is made
with a multitude of threads wound upon bobbins stuck in a pillow, so
that the lace is created in a range of twists and plaits combining a
varying number of threads, usually on a meshed ground. Where there
isn't a 'ground' ('fond' or 'reseau') the pattern is connected by
'brides' (bars or ties).

The centres for PILLOW LACE in England were Buckinghamshire,
Northamptonshire, Devonshire, Hertfordshire and Bedfordshire, but
lace has always been imported from abroad.

Most church lace is machine lace of the late 19th and early
20th centuries or 19th century hand-made lace applied to machine-
made net. Earlier laces, however, were given to churches at the end
of the 19th century and it is worth looking out for 17th century
needle laces and 18th century bobbin laces. If some lace does
appear to be of interest, the Victoria and Albert Museum will
advise.

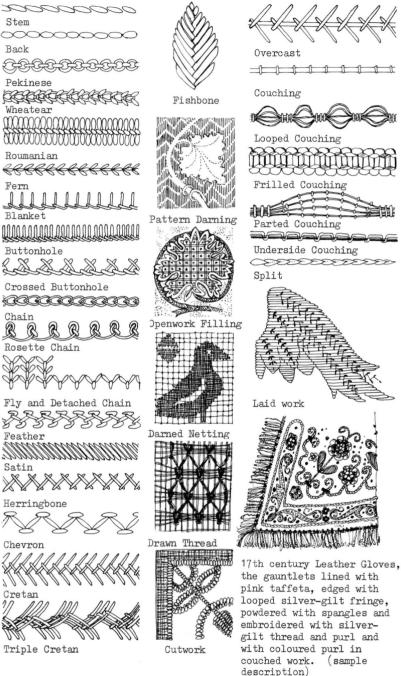

Stem

Back

Pekinese

Wheatear

Roumanian

Fern

Blanket

Buttonhole

Crossed Buttonhole

Chain

Rosette Chain

Fly and Detached Chain

Feather

Satin

Herringbone

Chevron

Cretan

Triple Cretan

Fishbone

Pattern Darning

Openwork Filling

Darned Netting

Drawn Thread

Cutwork

Overcast

Couching

Looped Couching

Frilled Couching

Parted Couching

Underside Couching

Split

Laid work

17th century Leather Gloves,
the gauntlets lined with
pink taffeta, edged with
looped silver-gilt fringe,
powdered with spangles and
embroidered with silver-
gilt thread and purl and
with coloured purl in
couched work. (sample
description)

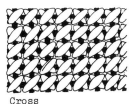

Cross

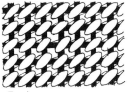

Tent

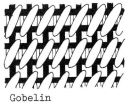

Gobelin

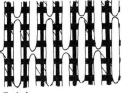

Irish

Italian

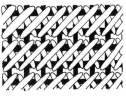

Plait

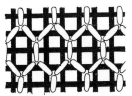

Holbein

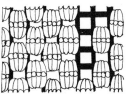

Rococo

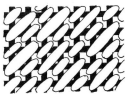

Mosaic

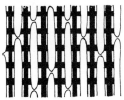

Florentine

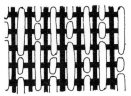

Parisian

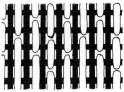

Hungarian

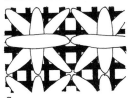

Smyrna

Rice

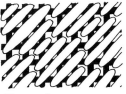

Diagonal

Eye

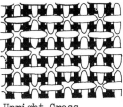

Upright Cross

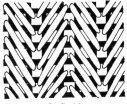

Diagonal Satin

LINEN   cloth woven from flax.
COTTON
VELVET   a pile fabric of silk, cotton, wool or synthetics.
DAMASK   self-coloured and patterned, silk or cotton.
               Linen-Damask may sometimes have woven dates, coats-of-
               arms, etc.
TAPESTRY   a woven technique and the term should never be used for
               canvas-work embroidery.
SILK   It is inadvisable to use the term 'Brocade' - it is
               preferable to describe an object as 'Green silk' or
               'Green silk damask, patterned with a large-scale floral
               design in coloured silks and metal threads'.
EMBROIDERY   Unless professional, a simple description of the ground
               fabric and the embroidery materials, together with
               details of the main colours and pattern, is adequate:
               'Canvas-work, a grey ground embroidered with keys of St
               Peter in red wool and some blue silk.'
               'Linen, embroidered with white linen thread in a variety
               of stitches and with additional open-work decoration,
               the main theme being the signs of the zodiac.'
LACE   see p.175.

GARNITURE   fringes, tassels, knots, cords, etc.
HERALDRY   adds historic interest to embroidery: the owners or
               donors may be traced by a coat-of-arms in the work.
FLOWERS, COLOURS and NUMBERS have symbolism and should be correctly
               described.
FIELD   is the term for 'background' - it is sometimes 'strewn'
               with flowers or other devices.
CLOTH of GOLD or of SILVER is fabric with gold or silver thread
               in-woven in the making.

GOLD EMBROIDERY is divided into three main classes:
               a. outline-work   is outlined with a couched gold
                                   cord or double thread.
               b. solid flat-work
               c. raised-work   - which introduces purls and bullions
                                   and the gold is applied to the
                                   material by some form of couching,
                                   sometimes with the help of a layer of
                                   linen.
               Goldwork may be   'Purl' - like a coiled spring, the
                                   larger sizes being termed 'bullion'.
                                   'Passing' - like gold wire.
                                   'Pearl Purl' - like tiny gold beads.
                                   'Plate' - flat strips.
                                   'Spangles' - thin pieces of pierced
                                   metal.

LUREX   20th century imitation gold thread.
SUEDE   much used in 20th century for appliqué.
BROCHE   a woven fabric with a pattern on the surface.

CREWEL WORK   is decorative work with coloured wools on a plain linen or twill ground.

APPLIED   is one material put onto another.

INLAID   is the fitting together of different pieces to form a pattern.

PATCHWORK   is similar to inlaid but usually symmetrically patterned.

QUILTING   is when more than two layers of material are kept together by a stitched pattern, with sometimes a cord inserted.

Quilting   Stumpwork

PHOTOGRAPHY   Colour photographs are not essential for textiles - the design and pattern are what are important. Illustrations should, if possible, show the entire object as well as additional photographs of details.

BIBLIOGRAPHY

DEAN, BERYL (1958), 'Ecclesiastical Embroidery', Batsford, London.
HANDS, M.H. (1957), 'Church Needlework', Faith Press, Leighton Buzzard.
Catalogues from Wippell Mowbray Church Furnishing Ltd, Newton Abbot.
'Encyclopaedia Britannica': Lace, Robes, Universities, Vestments, etc.

COPE of red silk damask with applied crimson velvet, gold braid,
green silk and canvas embroidered with gold thread, gold cord, and
silk in shades of green, red, yellow and brown, inlaid and couched
work with some nué and metal spangles.

The ground is powdered with fleurs-de-lys, sunbursts, stylised
pineapples and scrolled foliage and the letter 'P' surmounted by a
crown.

On the false orphreys are roundels containing at centre back a
Tudor rose and down the sides S P (for St Paul).

On the round hood, which is attached by five silk and gold thread
buttons and fringed with gold thread and red silk, is an applied
roundel with the Sacred Monogram 'ihc' within rays. The same device
appears on the morse.

ALB   Full length belted white tunic with narrow sleeves, possibly apparelled at neck and hem, or trimmed with a lace flounce in C of E, but only embroidered in RC. A ROCHET is similar but shorter, either sleeveless or sleeves gathered at wrist.

AMICE   White linen neck-cloth with an apparel at one edge.

APPAREL Decorated panel applied to dalmatics, albs and amices.

BIRETTA Black, purple, red or white ridged hat, worn according to rank, by priest, bishop, cardinal or pope.

CASSOCK Button-through gown, coloured according to rank as above, or of the colour of the habit of their order by monks.

CHASUBLE Circular or oval, with central head opening and orphreys, the principal vestment worn by an officiating priest.

COPE   Semicircular cape fastened with a morse, decorated with a hood and orphreys.

DALMATIC Sleeved, opensided tunic, worn by deacons, decorated with stripes called 'clavi' and sometimes with apparels.

GIRDLE   White or coloured cord belt with tassels.

HOOD   Flat vestigial hood attached to copes and also worn by scholars (see COSTUME).

LAPPETS Pair of 'ribbands' attached to the back of a mitre.

MANIPLE Decorated band worn over the arm - resembles a short stole - originally a towel and purse combined.

MITRE   Peaked headdress worn by bishops, pope and abbots: simplex= white; aurifrigiata=gold or silver on white; pretiosa=jewelled.

MORSE   Clasp used to fasten the cope - metal or embroidered.

MOZETTA Short hooded cape, buttoned down front, coloured as above.

ORPHREY Embroidered bands, usually applied, found on chasubles and copes. Orphreys on altar frontals are loose-hanging, otherwise the decoration is a 'panel'.

PALLIUM or PALL Originally a woollen vestment worn by archbishops, usually shown as a narrow Y-shaped strip, with embroidered crosses, falling down the centre front and back.

PASTORAL STAFF or CROZIER A stave, carried by high dignitaries, on which may be a cross, crook or horizontal crook (Tau-stave): sometimes a vexillium (scarf) is attached.

STOLE   Decorated band worn round the neck, beneath the chasuble, resembling, but longer than, the maniple: usually with a device at each end and at the neck.

SURPLICE White gown, differing from the alb by long flowing sleeves, worn over the cassock.

TIARA   Headdress of pope.

TUNICLE Similar to dalmatic, although longer when worn by bishops with a dalmatic: it has narrow sleeves and no apparels except occasionally near the neck: it is usually worn by sub-deacons.

Mitre

Pastoral Staff
or Crozier

Apparel of the
Amice

Episcopal Ring
(glove without
middle finger)

Pallium

Maniple

Chasuble

Dalmatic (fringed)

Tunicle

Stole

Apparel of the
Alb

Sandals

ARCHBISHOP

Flat Cap
Coif

Ruff

Bishop
sleeves
on the
Rochet

Chimère
(loose
sleeveless
gown)

Cassock
(purple)

17th century ARCHBISHOP

Scarlet
Skull Cap

White Collar
Blue Ribbon
on
Pectoral cross

Scarlet Cloak
with white-lined
shoulder Cape
(Mozetta)

Scarlet
Biretta

White Surplice
or Rochet

Cassock
(scarlet)

CARDINAL

Tonsure

Apparel of the
Amice

Chasuble
(Romanesque-
style)

Sleeves of
the Alb

Maniple

Orphrey of
the Chasuble

Stole

Apparel of
the Alb

PRIEST

Primitive style
DALMATIC
with clavi

Contemporary style
DALMATIC
with tassels and
clavi

The CHASUBLE
basically a cape with a hole in the centre,
has varied in shape throughout the centuries.
The authentic full tent-like form is usually
referred to as 'Romanesque'.

Gothic style,
with rounded hem and orphreys
embroidered in hand-worked appliqué
featuring Chi-Rho, Alpha and Omega and
ORPHREYS   Cross motifs. (sample description)

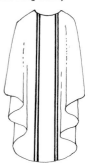

Pallium-shaped   Gothic Y-shaped   V-shaped   Pillar-shaped

Morse

Girdle of
the Alb

Orphrey of
the Cope

Apparel of
the Alb

Orphrey of
the Cope

Shield-
shaped Hood
with
applied
Sacred
Monogram
and Tassel

Apparel of
the Alb

COPE
featuring hand-
embroidered Maltese
Cross on a rounded
fringed hood, and
orphreys of contrasting
coloured velvet.

Cowl Hood

The COPE lends itself to the use of
beautiful materials and embroidery.
20th century designs are often hand-
worked in combinations of kid-leather,
beads, jewels, metallic threads, cords
and stitchery, and incorporate
imaginative use of symbols.

The MORSE, attached to the broad
fastening band across the chest,
may be embroidered or jewelled.

Lent/Advent Cope featuring
the Crown of Thorns,
Eclipse of the Sun and the
Star of Advent Motifs.

BIBLIOGRAPHY

CHRISTIE, A.H. (1906), 'Embroidery and Tapestry Weaving', John Hogg,
London.
DEAN, BERYL (1958), 'Ecclesiastical Embroidery', Batsford, London.
HANDS, M.H. (1957), 'Church Needlework', Faith Press, Leighton
Buzzard.
'Encyclopaedia Britannica': Lace, Robes, Universities, Vestments,
etc.
Catalogues from Wippell Mowbray Church Furnishing Ltd, Newton Abbot
will be found useful for beginners.

Comparison should be made with what has already been recorded and with what is still visible. The camera often picks out details not visible to the naked eye.

'FRESCO' is a technical term - all frescoes are murals (or wall paintings), but owing to dampness few frescoes have survived in England where the technique mostly used was 'SECCO', the early colours being confined to red, yellow, white and black - blue and green being rare.

Paintings were constantly replaced: during the Reformation all were obliterated and some overpainted with texts called 'SENTENCES'. Where the Victorians did not completely strip the walls, paintings may be found beneath layers of limewash or overpainting.

Subject matter was more important than artistic merit and few painters, except those working for royalty, are known. When deciphering the subject the paintings should be treated as 'strip cartoons'; they are sometimes in two or more tiers, the scenes being divided by architectural motifs or bordered top and bottom and running on like the Bayeux Tapestry: incidents are often telescoped. Sometimes figures at the end of one scene and the beginning of the next are back to back.

There are definite codes of signs. Good people have haloes, bad are caricatured, accessories are enlarged to emphasize rank, authority or cruelty. Costume is usually contemporary and important for dating work. Souls are depicted as naked figures but carry rank identifications - see sections on SAINTS and SIGNS AND SYMBOLS for the identification of figures and gestures.

Subject matter is grouped into
1 Decorative: Masonry pattern 12th-14th century, Scroll, Chevron,
                Heraldry, The Vine, both decorative and allegorical,
                Diapered backgrounds with small devices, which when
                they are clearly stencilled are usually 14th-15th
                century.
2 Bible stories, including the Tree of Life and Tree of Jesse.
3 Single figures of saints, apostles and martyrs and scenes from
   their lives.
4 Moralities or allegorical themes containing warnings against
   particular sins or modes of life, including the Seven Deadly
   Sins, the Seven Works of Mercy, the Weighing of Souls, The Doom
   or Last Judgment.

The general composition of The Doom is of Christ, robed to display the Five Wounds, seated on a rainbow, judging the quick and the dead: He blesses with one hand and holds up an open palm of judgment with the other: His feet rest on a sphere. He is flanked by groups of the Heavenly Host, Apostles, Evangelists, the Virgin Mary and John the Baptist. Angels bear Symbols of the Passion or blow trumpets. Scrolls often bear 'Come ye blessed of my Father, and inherit your kingdom' on His right hand, and on the other side 'Go ye evil doers into eternal fire'. Lower down is the General Resurrection with St Peter receiving the Blessed at the gate of the Heavenly Jerusalem, while the others are damned in Hell.

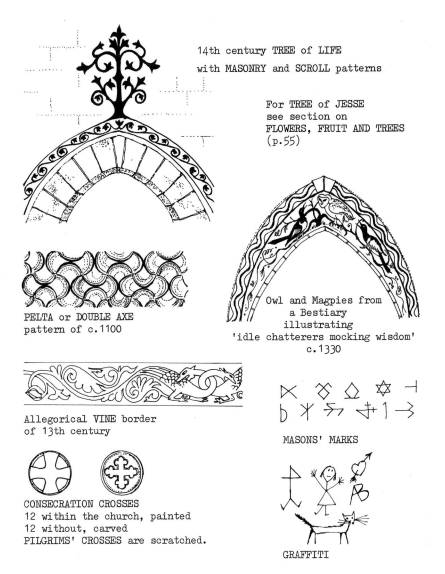

14th century TREE of LIFE
with MASONRY and SCROLL patterns

For TREE of JESSE
see section on
FLOWERS, FRUIT AND TREES
(p.55)

PELTA or DOUBLE AXE
pattern of c.1100

Owl and Magpies from
a Bestiary
illustrating
'idle chatterers mocking wisdom'
c.1330

Allegorical VINE border
of 13th century

MASONS' MARKS

CONSECRATION CROSSES
12 within the church, painted
12 without, carved
PILGRIMS' CROSSES are scratched.

GRAFFITI

BIBLIOGRAPHY

NEEDHAM, A. (1944), 'How to Study an Old Church', Batsford, London.
ROUSE, E.C. (1968), 'Discovering Wall Paintings' (with
acknowledgment for use of text), Shire Publications, Aylesbury.
WRIGHT, G.A.A. and WHEELER, W.A. (1971), 'Masons' Marks on Wells
Cathedral Church', Friends of Wells Cathedral, Wells.

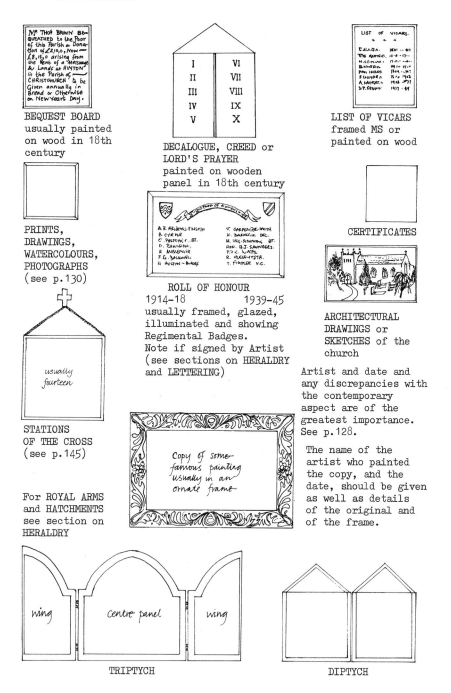

Mr THOS BROWN BE-
QUEATHED to the Poor
of this Parish a Dona-
tion of £210,0, Now
£8,15,0 arising from
the Rent of a "Messuage
& Lands at HINTON"
in the Parish of
CHRISTCHURCH" to be
Given annually in
Bread or Otherwise
on New Year's Day.

BEQUEST BOARD
usually painted
on wood in 18th
century

I	VI
II	VII
III	VIII
IV	IX
V	X

**DECALOGUE, CREED or
LORD'S PRAYER**
painted on wooden
panel in 18th century

LIST OF VICARS.

LIST OF VICARS
framed MS or
painted on wood

**PRINTS,
DRAWINGS,
WATERCOLOURS,
PHOTOGRAPHS**
(see p.130)

ROLL OF HONOUR

A.B. ... J. CARPENTER-SMITH
B. CARTER ... K. BARRCLIE. DFC.
C. PRETONE ... BT. M. ING-SINANNN. BT.
D. RANISION. HON. B.J. SAUNDERS.
E. MERENGER ... P.S.C. WATTS.
F.G. BALLWELL. ... R. HUSSE-4TSTA.
H. AUSTIN - BURGES ... T. FIDDLER V.C.

ROLL OF HONOUR
1914-18   1939-45
usually framed, glazed,
illuminated and showing
Regimental Badges.
Note if signed by Artist
(see sections on HERALDRY
and LETTERING)

CERTIFICATES

**ARCHITECTURAL
DRAWINGS or
SKETCHES** of the
church

Artist and date and
any discrepancies with
the contemporary
aspect are of the
greatest importance.
See p.128.

**STATIONS
OF THE CROSS**
(see p.145)

usually
fourteen

For ROYAL ARMS
and HATCHMENTS
see section on
HERALDRY

Copy of some
famous painting
usually in an
ornate frame

The name of the
artist who painted
the copy, and the
date, should be given
as well as details
of the original and
of the frame.

wing   centre panel   wing

TRIPTYCH

DIPTYCH

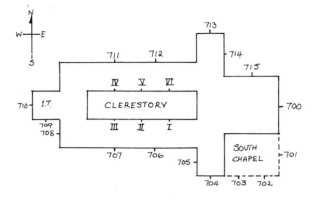

Draw a plan of the church (plans will be found in the RCHM or church leaflet) and number the windows. NADFAS members number the East Window, behind the altar, 700 and work clockwise in Arabic, using Roman for the Clerestory and suffixing a 'T' for Tower windows. The compass points should be given on the plan.

Draw a plan of EACH window. A tracing from a photograph is useful, but if not available a simple line drawing is adequate. Put the number of the window (from the church plan) and the location on the drawing - i.e. 706 in the above plan would be Nave S wall E - V would be Clerestory N wall centre. When referring to chapels use the compass points rather than 'Lady Chapel' or 'St Margaret's Chapel'.

Number every LIGHT on your separate window plans, across from left to right, starting at the top - see below the plan given with the sample description of one window. If the correct nomenclature of the tracery is known, it should be given with reference to the glossary used.

Describe what is to be seen by the numbers allocated, but using the SEQUENCE of numbers in the most CONVENIENT form - i.e. do the whole light downwards, or work across all the lights of the window as has been done in the sample.

If, in the sample window, the recorder had described the whole of the main left light before tackling the others, the numbering of the description would have read 11, 14, 17, 20. In some cases it will be simpler to work parts across the window and parts by lights - as long as it is CLEAR to the READER and the numbering is adhered to, it does not matter.

Having, presumably, first dealt with the Tracery Lights, the MAIN LIGHTS should be divided into sections, starting with the head, followed by the canopy (if any), then the subject, figures and background, then the odd panel at the bottom and the Inscription or Dedication. The TEXTS will have been dealt with in the appropriate places, or, if preferred, briefly referred to on site and given in whole at the end of the description.

The correct naming of Saints and Biblical figures or Biblical Scenes is important (see section on SAINTS AND SCENES).

As for tracery terms, if the correct names for parts of costumes are known, use should be made of them, but reference to the glossary used should be added (see section on COSTUME).

Colours should be described in primary tones, not in the recorder's idea of 'slatey blue' or 'cabbage green'. A general overall description such as 'bright and cheerful' or 'subdued tones' is acceptable, but value judgments such as 'pretty' or 'moving' should be avoided.

Texts and inscriptions should be given fully, although if the text has been executed correctly the chapter and verse in the Bible will suffice. Note should be made of the style of lettering, the arrangement of lines, all contractions and abbreviations (see section on LETTERING).

Details of LEADING should be ignored unless really significant.

Lights made up of a haphazard medley of fragments of mediaeval glass should be described as such, only mentioning pieces of interest.

If no record of the date of a window can be found, a guess may be hazarded, but the fact that it is a 'guess' should be stated and possibly the reason for making it, even if it is only the date of the masonry surrounding the window or that some of the clear glass quarries are of different texture from the rest.

Describe, and give the whereabouts of any signature and the location number in the appropriate light. The use of the word 'MARK' will disguise the fact that the recorder does not know whether it belongs to the artist who painted the glass, the designer or the workshop where it was assembled.

Certain workshops used standard models of saints, Roman soldiers, monograms and even musical instruments played by angels, so the accuracy of descriptions can be of help to others making specific researches. If possible make a tracing or drawing of monograms.

PHOTOGRAPHY - Both the above details and a photograph of every window is essential. They are complementary to each other.

Photographers are advised not to use flash and to avoid strong sunlight. The architectural tracery details are seen better from a photograph taken from outside the church.

Places for Reference:
The Incumbent, Minutes of the Parish Councils and the Parish Magazines.
Diocesan Registry and the County Records Office.
The 'Builder' and the 'Ecclesiologist', Kendrick's Records and various records of commissions at the Victoria & Albert Museum, Society of Antiquaries in Burlington House, London and The Ely Stained Glass Museum (Curator, Martin Harrison).
Council for Care of Places of Worship, London Wall.

The largest area of this light, as now assembled, is taken up by a series of rectangular pictures set in elaborate frames of ornamental strapwork and ranged in units of six or eight, each unit surmounted by shallow intersecting ogee arches squared up to make rectangular panels.

The arched head of the window has in the centre a coat of arms within a wreath of leaves and a rectangular frame. Surmounting and flanking it is a medley of disparate figures, birds, fishes and other decorative devices, many incomplete, leaded up into a bizarre patchwork.

The pictorial panels are painted in brilliant colours and have a scrollwork setting.

The pattern of the leads is from Walter Gedde's 'Booke of Sundry Draughtes' (1615).

The painter of the panels made use of engravings for his subject matter, in some cases virtually the whole print was copied but in others only some small part was used.
(Plagiarism of this kind was very common in the 16th and 17th centuries.)

Sources much used were

a set of birds by A. Collaert, 'Avium Vivae Icones';
fishes by J. Sadeler, 'Piscium Vivae Icones';
Ovid's 'Metamorphoses' by A. Tempesta (1606);
sets of flowers by J. Sadeler, 'Florae Deae' and Crispin van de Passe's 'Hortus Floridus' (1614);
animals from Conrad Gessner's 'Icones Animalium' (1560), A. Collaert's and M. Gerardo's 'Animalium Quadrupedum' and A. Tempesta's 'Fighting Animals' (1600);
figures from Jost Amman's 'Kunstbuchlein' (1599) and from prints by J. Saenredam after H. Goltzius (1569).

Acknowledgment for the above is made to Michael Archer, Beest, Bird or Flower, Stained Glass. 'Country Life', 3 June 1976.

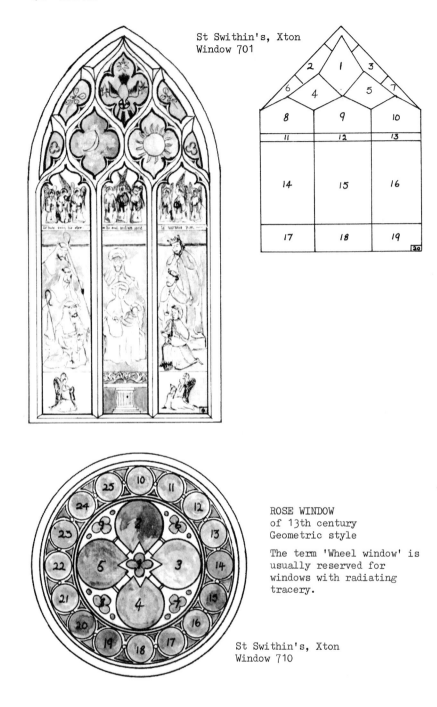

St Swithin's, Xton
Window 701

ROSE WINDOW
of 13th century
Geometric style

The term 'Wheel window' is
usually reserved for
windows with radiating
tracery.

St Swithin's, Xton
Window 710

701. Late 19th century window   S Chapel E
      of three trefoil headed lights
      with 14th century Reticulated style Tracery
      (ref: Harris and Lever)

NATIVITY Clear bright colours.

MARK of a daisy within a bell for Margaret Bell in 20.
Faculty with design, dated 10 June 1891 in Rectory.

1   Dove descending amidst three stars in purple night sky.
2 & 3 A sprig of oak leaves with acorn in natural colouring
    against a light yellow ground.
4   Crescent moon against dark blue sky.
5   Sun against light blue sky.
6 & 7 In each a trefoil lined out in black against a pale yellow
    ground.
8, 9 & 10 In each three angels in white girdled tunics, the centre
    ones playing a musical instrument, rebec, harp and tabor,
    the outer ones all singing. Multicoloured wings.
11, 12 & 13 Text: 'We have seen his star/in the east and are come/
                    to worship him'
    Black 19th century Gothic caps and smalls on a pale yellow
    ground, difficult to read but enough to identify with
    Matthew II.2.
14 Three shepherds, placed vertically, the top one standing, the
    lowest one kneeling, all with nomads' headdresses, each in a
    different brightly coloured cloak, red, yellow and blue; two
    hold crooks, the kneeling shepherd does not appear to have one.
15 VM seated with babe on knee and Joseph standing behind.
    Joseph in dark red cloak and yellow numbus.   VM in royal blue
    mantle with gold trimming. Babe swaddled.
16 Three kings, similarly placed to the shepherds: Caspar in
    purple robe with fur cape-collar attached with a tied chain,
    Melchior in rich brown robe, the younger kneeling Balthasar in
    white tunic and emerald green super tunic, with his crown on
    the ground, is bearing a gift.
        A plain silver dado behind all three scenes, with light blue
    sky above.
17 & 19 A kneeling angel in each, both with flame coloured wings
    and nimbi, yellow stain ground.
18 An Old Testament 'Altar of Sacrifice' in natural colours
    against a green ground.
20 Artist's signature.

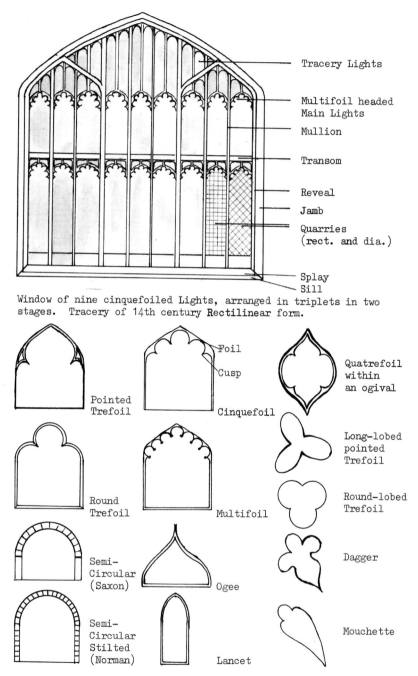

Tracery Lights

Multifoil headed
Main Lights

Mullion

Transom

Reveal

Jamb

Quarries
(rect. and dia.)

Splay
Sill

Window of nine cinquefoiled Lights, arranged in triplets in two
stages.   Tracery of 14th century **Rectilinear** form.

Pointed
Trefoil

Foil

Cusp

Cinquefoil

Quatrefoil
within
an ogival

Round
Trefoil

Multifoil

Long-lobed
pointed
Trefoil

Round-lobed
Trefoil

Semi-
Circular
(Saxon)

Ogee

Dagger

Semi-
Circular
Stilted
(Norman)

Lancet

Mouchette

Norman

Lancet

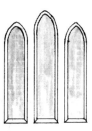

Grouped Lancets

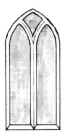

13th century
Y-tracery

13th century
Plate

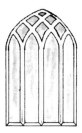

13th century
Intersected

13th century
Geometrical

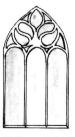

13th and 14th
century
Curvilinear
or Flowing

14th century
Reticulated

14th century
Drop

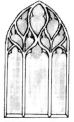

14th century
Flamboyant

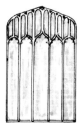

15th century
Rectilinear, Panel
or Perpendicular

CANOPY | A background of turrets, niches, arcades, above or around the figures or in the tracery.

CUSP | A projection carved on the underside of an arch. Cusps divide the underside into a series of 'foils' or arcs and are purely ornamental; they are moulded and sometimes terminate in a flower.

DEDICATION | Devout inscription.

ENAMELLING | The grinding of glass to a fine powder and mixing with a fusible liquid and applying it to white glass, from which it tends to flake - a method used during the Reformation.

GRISAILLE | Yellow, grey or brown monochromatic colouring used from 13th century (not to be confused with 'yellow stain') with a pattern. It is advisable to describe 19th and 20th century copies as 'plain glass quarries painted or pressed with ....'

HACHURES | Small shading lines.

HERALDIC ARMS | should be blazoned unless well known (see section on HERALDRY).

INSCRIPTION | When describing windows this term is usually reserved for the bare mention of the donor or event comemorated.

LIGHTS | Main Lights are the sections of windows divided by Transoms or Mullions. Tracery Lights are the sections in the ornamental tracery formed by the branching of mullions in the upper part of a window; the very small pieces are called 'eyelets'. Blind tracery is self-descriptive.

LINED OUT | in black paint or enamel means 'drawn in'.

QUARRIES | Any regular form of square or diamond shaped glass.

STAINED GLASS | A misleading term - the only colour that can be obtained by staining is yellow.

TEXTS | Quotations from the Bible.

BIBLIOGRAPHY

HAHNLOSER, HANS R., ed., 'Corpus Vitrearum Medii Aevi', Unesco, on which system the above has been based, as kindly interpreted by Mr Michael Archer, Keeper of the Department of Ceramics, Victoria & Albert Museum, London, February 1976.
HARRIS, J. and LEVER, J. (1966), 'Illustrated Glossary of Architecture 850-1830', Faber & Faber, London.
HARRISON, K. (1965), 'An Illustrated Guide to the Windows of King's College Chapel Cambridge', printed for the College.
KIRBY, A.T. (1952), The Stained Glass Artist - His Mark, 'Journal of the British Society of Master Glass Painters', vol.X, no.4, pp.205-12.

See also sections on COSTUME, HERALDRY, MUSICAL INSTRUMENTS, SAINTS, SCENES, SIGNS AND SYMBOLS, etc.

Thomas of
Oxford

Christopher
Webb

Geoffrey Webb

John Thornton

Robert L. Hendra
and Geoffrey F.
Harper

Paul Woodruffe

Powell & Sons
of Whitefriars

J.E. Nutgens

Charles E. Kempe

Walter E. Tower

Francis W.
Skeat

Francis W.
Skeat

Francis W. Skeat

W. Holland
Warwick

William
Warrington

M.E. Aldrich
Rope

Drake of Exeter

Reginald Bell

Clayton & Bell

Thomas
Willement

John Clement Bell

Alfred Bell

M. Farrar Bell

William
Wailes

C.C. Townsend
and J. Howson

Goddard & Gibbs

Rachel de
Montmorency

Hugh Easton

Walter
Wilkinson

J.W. Kubler

E.F. Brickdale

Edward Jenkins
Prest

J.N. Comper

H.W. Bryans

Martin Travers

T. Salusbury

Peter Cole

Martin Webb

John Lawson
(Goddard & Gibbs)

C. Rupert Moore

Percy Bacon
and Brothers

Lawrence S. Lee

pre 1970

post 1970

Wippell Mowbray Church
Furnishing Ltd

Ray Bradley

Shrigley
& Hunt

Henry James
Salisbury

N.H.J. Westlake

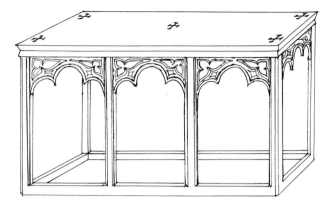

19th and 20th century style purpose-built ALTAR.

Rectangular frame with plain table-top, incised with five
Consecration Crosses, set on a projecting cornice.

Front divided into three bays, the back open.

Sides and each bay of the front contain, at the top, brackets
pierced with shaped trefoil and lozenge tracery and shaped on the
outside to resemble cusped round Gothic arches.

Most of the members of the framework, which stands on a base of
rails, are chamfered on the outside.

Similar constructions, usually hidden by the frontal, often have
the fronts and sides panelled with applied Gothic tracery, the back
being left open.

The term BENCHES is here applied to wooden seating other than
elevated or enclosed seating such as box pews or squire and family
pews.

BENCHES consist of seats with supports, backs with open rails or
panels, bookrests either sloping or level (mediaeval bookrests are
always level, post Reformation usually sloping), fitted to the backs
for the use of occupants of the bench behind. To each section of
benching there is usually a BENCH FRONT or DESK and care should be
taken when counting to separate Benches from Desks (to complicate
counting there is sometimes a bench-seat attached to the front of
the Front!). Bench-ends are important and note should be made of
their shape, carving and finials, usually called poppyheads.

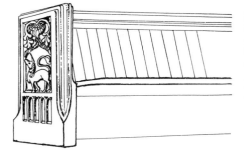

BENCH with panelled back,
moulded top rail and
curved seat.
Carved rectangular bench-
end, the lower third with
a gouged blind arcade, the
upper part showing a
Unicorn gazing at a
stylised pomegranate.

Bench Front with integral
kneeler and level bookrest.
Rectangular arch-topped end
with lively 16th century
carving and fleur-de-lys
poppyhead. The desk
supported on a colonnade of
trefoil headed arches with
pierced triangular spandrels.

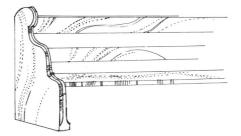

Open-backed BENCH with two
rails and shaped end with
simply moulded edging, the
other end of the bench
flush with wall.

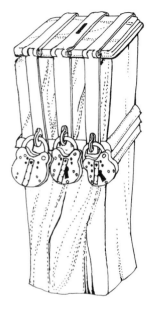

17th century POOR BOX

formed from hollowed out oak post.
Lid, with coin slot, has three iron straps
hinged at the front and secured to the
post by padlocks.
Simple applied moulding around three sides.

FERETORY

A shrine for
a saint's
relics.

A metal rod across the
roofed top secures the
hasp and has eyelets for
attaching the priest's
neck-cord.
Pierced round and
rectangular apertures in
roof and sides.

16th century ALMS BOX, Oak
Rectangular with rounded lid, bound
with iron straps and decorated with
enamel tracery.

17th century ALMS BOX, Oak
Rectangular box with carved inscription on
the front 'REMEMBER THE PORE' in Roman caps
and the date '1684' above in Arabic figures,
supported on acanthus leaf bracket which is
dated 1844 at the top R corner.

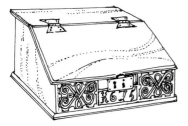

17th century DESK-type BIBLE BOX

with butterfly hinges.
Typical Lake District style
interlace carving on the front
flanking the keyplate below
which is the date 1675.
Neatly moulded edges. Oak.

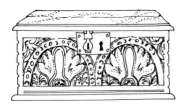

17th century Rectangular BIBLE BOX

with original lock and hasp.
Two large lunettes carved on
front enclosing stylised leaf
decoration and similar motifs
in the spandrels.

20th century Book of Remembrance
STAND

Desk top with glazed viewing
panel, supported on a metal
frame of a pair of standards
fixed to the rear base of the
desk, the feet curving forward
to take the balance; two
stretchers unite the standards.

20th century Book of Remembrance
STAND

Table style with glazed top to
box which has an acanthus
scrolled frieze of applied
carving. An apron below the
box has pierced quatrefoil
carving and a blank shield at
centre front.
A shelf unites the four legs of the
square section.

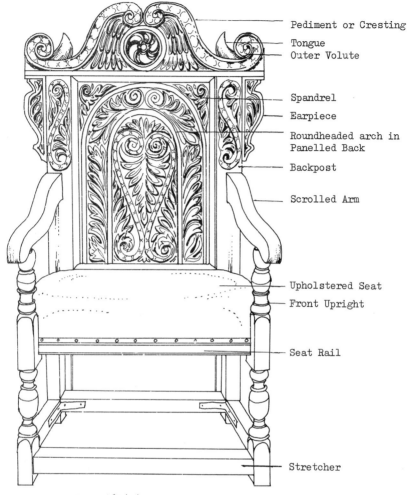

Pediment or Cresting

Tongue
Outer Volute

Spandrel

Earpiece

Roundheaded arch in
Panelled Back

Backpost

Scrolled Arm

Upholstered Seat

Front Upright

Seat Rail

Stretcher

Yorkshire 1625-50

Oak.   Panel back construction.   Panel carved with a roundheaded arch
decorated with scrolled foliage.   Scrolled pediment, with tongues
protruding beside outer volutes, carved with foliage and a central
roundel.   Carving similar to that on the back on earpieces and backposts above the scrolled arms.   Turned front uprights of baluster
form.   Seat upholstered in red figured velvet with various
reinforcements.   Plain renewed stretchers.

N.B.   In chairs of this type, the backs are sometimes raked
(sloped), seats splayed, stretchers and front uprights vary in form.

See sections on STRETCHERS, LEGS and FEET.

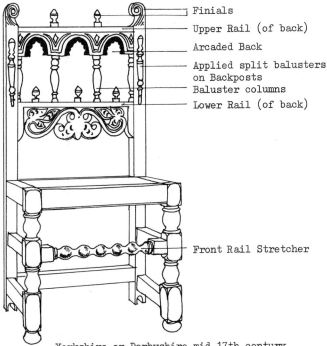

Finials

Upper Rail (of back)

Arcaded Back

Applied split balusters
on Backposts
Baluster columns

Lower Rail (of back)

Front Rail Stretcher

Yorkshire or Derbyshire mid 17th century

Arcaded back, the upper rail having three arches with carved
and incised decoration and cusping supported by two baluster
columns resting on a lower rail with leafy scrolls; the upper
rail surmounted by two, and the lower by three knob finials.
The back uprights have crozier-shaped finials and applied split
baluster ornaments. Spirally turned front rail stretcher, the
rest plain. Front legs have new feet: back legs slotted for
castors. Seat sunk for a squab cushion.

Glastonbury Chair c.1630
(much copied in 19th century)

The term 'Glastonbury' denotes a
panel-backed chair, the X-shaped
legs joined by a crossbar and held
by wooden pins and the shaped arms
united to the back and seat in the
same way.
The only description required,
beyond 'Glastonbury', is of the rake
of the back, the shape of the arms
and the decoration which may be on
both the inside and rear of the back
and arms, the wood, date and
measurements.

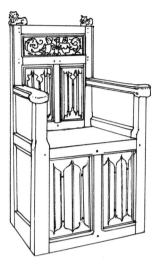

The upper part of the square back,
which is surmounted at either end
by the figure of a crouching lion,
has an oblong panel of finely carved
Renaissance design consisting of a
male and female terminal figure
supporting a trophy of arms, their
tails ending in scrolls. Below it
are two linenfold panels. The flat
arms are enclosed with plain panels.
The lower part of the back is fitted
behind with a cupboard door.
The front of the box has two linenfold panels of simpler design than
those of the back.

Oak Armchair of Box Form
Cambridgeshire c.1530

Flat pyramidal caps to backposts.
Lunette cresting carved with a
tulip amidst sprawling foliage.

Similar carving on panel with a
dog-rose.

Opening below panel.

Grooved seat rails.

Turned front legs.
Bobbin-turned front rail stretcher.

Panel-back construction c.1660

Top rail of back
treated with
lunettes.

Lozenge carving in
4-panelled back.

Jacobean Oak SETTLE
First half of 17th century

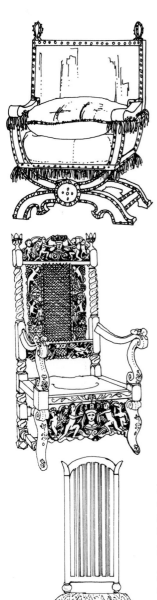

CHAIR OF STATE c.1600

Armchair of horizontal X-frame
construction, closely covered in
crimson velvet, trimmed with fringed
gold gallon and garnished with gilt
headed nails and fitted with down
stuffed cushion covered en suite.

Walnut ARMCHAIR c.1670

The cresting of the back and of the
rail joining the front cabriole legs is
elaborately carved in openwork with
cherubs crowning a woman and a cherub
blowing a trumpet on either side.

The spiral uprights have crowned female
head finials. Upon each armrest is a
lion couchant.

The sides of the back are adorned with
openwork carvings of cherubs amidst vines
and roses growing up from baskets. The
back has the original canework; the
seat, formerly caned, is upholstered in
green velvet.

Beech c.1690

Tall back with moulded arched cresting
rail, with ears, and a straight lower back
rail enclosing five vertical moulded spars.

Front seat rail has veneered and shaped
apron, hidden by fringe of red Victorian
plush covering the slightly tapering seat.

The turned front legs, with ball feet, are
united by a turned front stretcher rail.
Turned H stretchers unite all four legs,
the back legs being slightly splayed.

The mouldings where the back uprights join
the cresting rail have been carefully
mitred at each corner.

Mid 19th century
Shouldered balloon HALLCHAIR
of X construction.

The rococo 'S' scrolls of the
back and the X tied with acanthus.

Heavily grooved seat rails.

On the back is a fragmentary label,
probably from an auction catalogue,
stating that the chair once stood in
the hall of Fawley Castle.

Beech CHURCH CHAIR of 19th and 20th
centuries
mostly made in Buckinghamshire.

Top rail usually shaped
Middle rails often bowed
Saddle seat (sometimes rush seats)
Book pocket between backposts
Box stretchers with attached shelf
for kneeler.

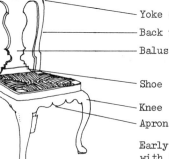

Yoke or top or cresting rail
Back upright
Baluster or Vase splat

Shoe

Knee
Apron

Early 18th century bended back SIDE CHAIR
with flowing cresting rail, cabriole
front legs, wavy apron and no
underpinning. The seat is rushed.

English WINDSOR CHAIRS come in many shapes and usually, though not always, have ELM seats, BEECH spindles (struts, stays or rods), BEECH legs and stretchers, and ASH bowed parts.

The legs and supports are pegged into the seat, the legs being splayed. Sometimes two stays form a brace from the top of the back to a bobtail projecting from the rear of the seat. A horizontal hoop forms a semi-circle across the back and along to the front as arm supports - if the hoop is missing and the back bowed, the chair is known as 'single-bowed Windsor'. Each style has a name, comb, fan, arched, squared, scrolled, etc.

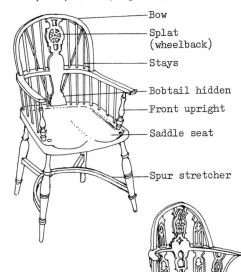

———— Bow

———— Splat
       (wheelback)

———— Stays

———— Bobtail hidden

———— Front upright

———— Saddle seat

———— Spur stretcher

Smoker's Bow c.1860
with double H stretcher

18th century Yew-wood
armchair of Gothick
Windsor type with arch
bow, ash saddle seat,
cabriole legs, club feet,
crinoline (spur) stretcher
and turned back supports.

19th century Mendlesham type Windsor
Low back with double
crest rail of square
section infilled with
three turned balls.
Ornamented splat with
three sticks each side.
Flat outward curving
arms extending beyond
sloping supports.
Saddle seat, splayed legs
and H stretcher.

Lathe back Windsor

Hoop back
Windsor

Gothick
Hoop back Windsor

Low back Windsor

Comb back Windsor

Tablet back Windsor

High back
Ladderback Windsor

Gothick Revival

Romantic Revival

mid 18th century
Oval

Balloon

Shouldered Balloon

Spoon

Queen Anne

Fiddle

Lyre

Ribband

Shield

Square

Prince of Wales
Feathers

Ladder

Abbotsford

19th century Gothic

19th century Elizabethan

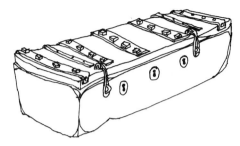

Mediaeval DUGOUT

Hollowed log with solid
slab lid, strengthened by
iron bands and strap hinges.
Provision for three locks
and padlock loops.

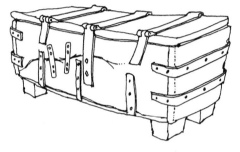

14th–16th centuries

Massive planks pegged into
posts of square section,
raising the chest from
floor, strengthened by
angled iron straps: flat
straps strengthen the breaks
in the timber. Strap hinges
continue across the top and
are hinged to the hasps of
the locks.

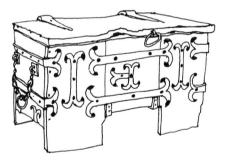

Early 14th century

Front and back tenoned into
wide stiles which are
extended to provide legs.
Iron straps, binding the
chest, have bifurcated ends
forming decoration.
Sides have chains with rings
suspended from them.

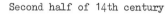

Second half of 14th century

Front of two vertical stiles
and two horizontal planks.
'Flanders' chests appears to
have been a generic term
referring to tracery-fronted
chests.
Traces of painted decoration
in the fantastic bestiary
scenes on the stiles.

15th century COFFER
for valuables

Tapering towards back and
base, bound in a grid of
straight and scrolled straps
with incised designs.
Lid, at wider end of top,
pivoting on three hinges is
pierced with coin slots.
Large handles at each end.

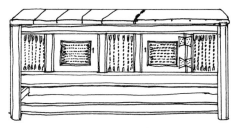

Early 17th century HUTCH

Frame and panel construction.
The five panels at front and
back and the two on the
sides are decorated with
simple linenfold, the
arrises of which are gouged
in a series of V-shaped cuts.
Two stretchers run the
length. Original doors
fastened to frame. Top sawn
and hinged to provide access.

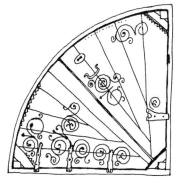

13th century COPE CHEST

Quadrant shape with frame of
stout posts at corners into
which rails are tenoned.
Lid in two halves with
ornate scrolled and foliated
hinges and decoration.
Panels of sides nailed into
rebates in frame.

h. 75 cm   dia. 198 cm

Early 17th century
DOLE CUPBOARD

Enclosed by two doors, each
having six turned spindles
in two stages.
Pilasters carved with stiff
leaves.
Geometric inlay on frieze.
Stamped enrichment on
cornice.

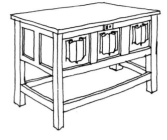

16th century COUNTER

Chest with fairly long
legs, about table height,
the top sometimes
scored.

17th century MULE CHEST

Shallow type of panelled
chest with drawers in
lower part.

Made until c.1800

**Late 18th century mahogany
CHEST OF DRAWERS**

The serpentine front with
cross-banded canted
corners. Cockbeading on
the fronts of the three
drawers. Brass swan-
necked handles and
C-scrolled keyhole
escutcheons. A slide
above the top drawer.
Splayed feet.
Bow-shaped frieze.
(sample description)

Mid 19th century walnut DAVENPORT

with scrolled front uprights supporting
a scrolled flap.
Four drawers on left side and a cupboard
door concealing three drawers on other
side. Ink drawer on left. Bun feet.
(sample description - no need to explain
more of the construction as the name
Davenport is sufficient)

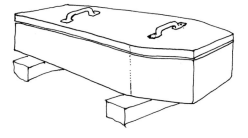

18th century MORTSAFE

Earlier ones usually
of stone and seldom
found with a lid.

19th and 20th
century
FRONTAL CHEST

Usually Deal.

Hinged top opening to enable
frontals to be hung on rods.
Approximately
105 cm h. x 300 w. x 30 d.

19th and 20th century
LINEN AND VESTMENT PRESS

Usually of Deal.

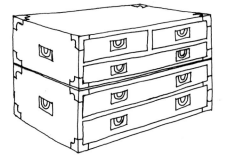

19th century MILITARY CHEST

In two stages with brass
corners and sunken
handles: no protrusions:
usually mahogany.
Sometimes the upper stage
is a secretaire.

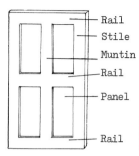

Rail
Stile
Muntin
Rail
Panel
Rail

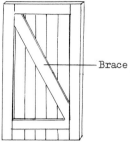

Brace

Ledge
Brace

Framed and Braced

Ledged and Braced

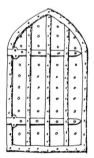

Saxon doors were stout defences made of thick oak boards placed vertically on the outside and horizontally inside, showing toolmarks and fastened together by long wrought-iron nails with ornamental heads, driven through and clenched on the inside.

Norman doors were decorated, sometimes on both sides, by the smith with wrought-iron hinges, locks, handles and knockers. The hinges usually have bi-furcated ends and stamped work of contemporary design.
It is difficult to differentiate between 19th century copies and original although the copies are usually more precise.

See 'hinges' in METALWORK section.

In the 14th century the decoration of doors passed to the carpenter, the smith's craft not reappearing until the late 17th century. Locks and hinges were plainer. Besides mouldings to cover the joints, tracery was either carved into the woodwork or applied with glue and nails.

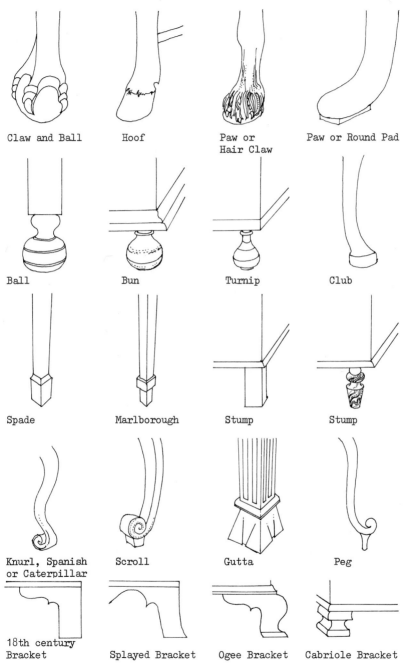

Claw and Ball

Hoof

Paw or
Hair Claw

Paw or Round Pad

Ball

Bun

Turnip

Club

Spade

Marlborough

Stump

Stump

Knurl, Spanish
or Caterpillar

Scroll

Gutta

Peg

18th century
Bracket

Splayed Bracket

Ogee Bracket

Cabriole Bracket

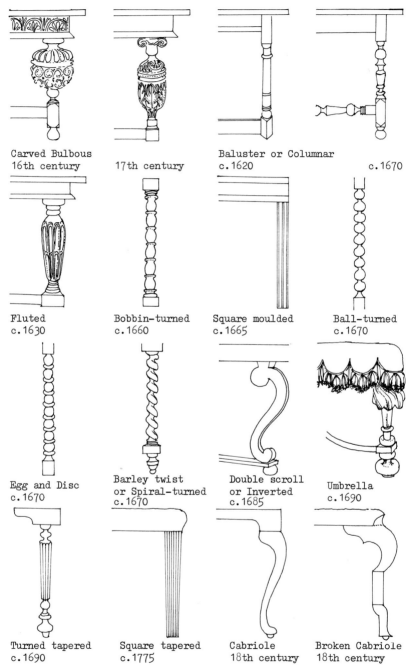

Carved Bulbous
16th century

17th century

Baluster or Columnar
c.1620

c.1670

Fluted
c.1630

Bobbin-turned
c.1660

Square moulded
c.1665

Ball-turned
c.1670

Egg and Disc
c.1670

Barley twist
or Spiral-turned
c.1670

Double scroll
or Inverted
c.1685

Umbrella
c.1690

Turned tapered
c.1690

Square tapered
c.1775

Cabriole
18th century

Broken Cabriole
18th century

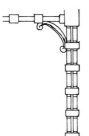

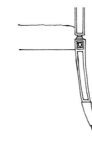

Cluster column
or Grouped pillar
c.1760

Applied fret
c.1765

Pierced fret

Sabre
c.1815

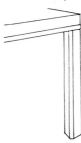

Hipped Cabriole
18th century

Reeded columnar
c.1803

Vase-shaped
slab standard or
trestle

Square
chamfered on
inside

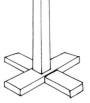

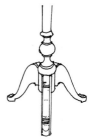

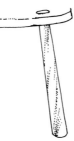

Fluted vase stem
pre 1800

Cruciform

Tripod foot on
stem

Splayed

FONT COVER

of three stages.

Highest stage: lofty crocketed pinnacle
with gables at base and finial top,
supported on five slender annulated columns.

Middle stage: cruciform in plan, with four
slender annulated compound columns at centre,
flanked by eight slender annulated columns in
pairs supporting a roof with four projecting
crocketed gables.

Lowest stage: square in plan: at each angle
flying diagonal buttresses culminating in
crocketed pinnacles: at each side a panel
carved with two foliage filled quatrefoils below, and above, an open pointed arch with bead
moulding on the extrados and enclosing
geometrical tracery, supported on slender
central annulated columns; the crown of the
arch breaking into a crocketed gable with a
pierced trefoil in its upper angle.
Inside, painted figures of Christ kneeling
and John the Baptist standing.

Base with a band of moulding formed from a
geometrical pattern of mostly circular
indentations, and with a band of imbricated
decoration inclined inwards.

The contraption to lift such a cover is called a FONT CRANE.

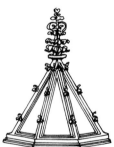

CONE COVER

six-sided
and
enclosed
with
crocketed
straight
ribs.

CROWN COVER

with open ogee
trusses above a
shallow enclosed
hexagonal-sided
drum

Turned baluster
central shaft

Bulb finial

CONSOLE

The frame of an
organ, containing
the keyboards,
stops, etc. as
illustrated

BALDACHINO
(known also as a Ciborium)

CONSOLE

Table supported by
a bracket against
a wall

CONSOLE

Mirror supported
by a bracket
against a wall

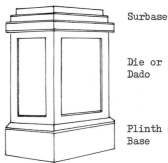

Surbase

Die or
Dado

Plinth or
Base

PEDESTAL

On a wall dado, the
horizontal base member
is called 'skirting'

CONSOLE

Any bracket or
corbel of
scrolled form

BRACKET

Pierced and
pinnacled
BRACKET
in the form of
a flying
buttress

Romayne
c.1530

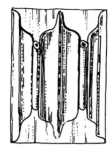

Parchment
early 16th century

Linenfold
early 16th century

Gothic (pierced)
early 16th century

Renaissance
mid 16th century

Gothic (pierced)
typical 16th century

Fielded (raised)
from 18th century

Coffered (sunk)
from 18th century

Applied Gothic
Tracery, usually
19th or 20th century

PANELS are always bevelled or rebated, so as to produce a border;
if they are flush, beading is added to conceal the join. All the
above styles, especially the Linenfold, have been much copied.

WAINSCOT is the term now used for most wooden panelling on walls:
its earlier use was for oakwood wagon boarding and old inventories
refer to wainscot chests or tables.

DADO is the term used for wood or coloured facing of the lower few
feet (or cm) of a room wall or pedestal.

The term PEW is reserved here for boxed seating, consisting of
panelling, doors and benches. Some pews are raised above floor
level, are canopied, furnished and heated; some have the names of
houses or families, or coats-of-arms, painted or carved on them.
Most are of oak until the 19th century and from then of oak or pine.

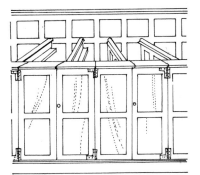

Early 17th century BOX PEWS

18th century BOX PEWS

STALLS are individual or multiple seats placed against a wall or
screen and sometimes 'returned' (at right angles). Some have
tabernacled canopies, or traceried backs and cornices; nearly all
have shaped side-panelling, some with carved or applied elbows.
The stall fronts (or desks) may be traceried and have poppyheads.

MISERICORDS (tip-up seats) usually have interesting carving, the
subsidiary carvings on either side of the main projection being
known as 'supporters'.

STALLS of four Bays

with a Canopy formed
of a cusped ogee arch
over each stall,
decorated with flame-
like crockets and
fleur-de-lys finials
and supported by
turned shafts on the
arm rests.

Moulded scrolled
Elbows.

Misericords, carved on
the undersides with....
(sample description)

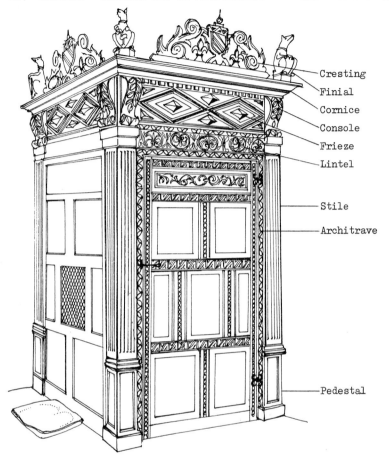

Cresting

Finial

Cornice

Console

Frieze

Lintel

Stile

Architrave

Pedestal

SHRIVING PEW, possibly adapted from an Elizabethan internal porch,
of square frame and panel construction of armoire style, with
reeded stiles of pilaster form mounted on pedestals with coffered
dado panels. The rails of the door carved with a geometric lined
motif, the muntins and stiles with guilloche, the architrave with
irregular chevrons, the fielded panels plain except for the horizontal top panel which bears a foliated scroll carving tied at the
centre. There is large palmette carving on the lintel and the
console brackets supporting the entablature are carved with leaves,
the frieze is enriched with mitred lozenge moulding surmounted by
dentil moulding, the latter omitted on the sides of the pew.

The sides do not have any enrichment other than fielded panels
below the frieze and consoles: on one side is a metal grille set
in a panel at eye-level for someone kneeling.

Above the moulded cornice are dog-like corner finials, squatting
on square plinths and holding shields between their paws:
crestings of coats-of-arms amidst floriated scrolls and fleurs-de-
lys are set between them.

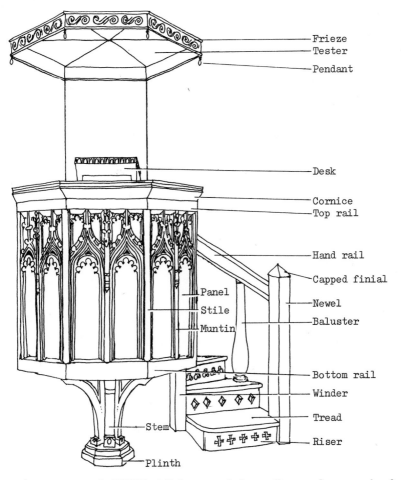

Frieze
Tester
Pendant

Desk

Cornice
Top rail

Hand rail
Capped finial
Panel
Stile
Newel
Muntin
Baluster

Bottom rail
Winder
Tread
Stem
Riser
Plinth

15th century oak PULPIT with hexagonal drum, the panels on each of
the four facets richly carved with blind tracery and cinquefoil ogee
arches, crockets and finials, the two arches on each panel separated
by small buttresses on the muntins.

19th century stem (pillar or post) with attached brackets on
hexagonal plinth.

19th century hexagonal tester with pendant finials at each angle
and a frieze of scrolled carving.

Desk made from a piece of 15th or 16th century oak with gouged
edges.

19th century stairway of four treads on S side, each riser pierced
with a set of five crosses, lozenges, trefoils or quatrefoils in
ascending order. Plain rectangular newel post with pyramidal capped
finial, a grooved hand rail and one strangely shaped baluster.

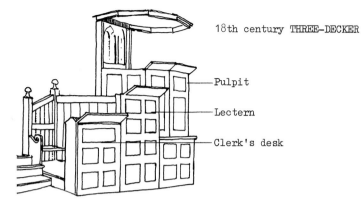

18th century THREE-DECKER

Pulpit

Lectern

Clerk's desk

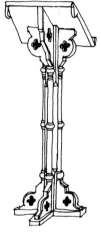

19th century oak LECTERN (for other Lecterns see METALWORK section)

Desk supported on solid cruciform brackets with shaped and bevelled edges, each bracket pierced in the centre with a quatrefoil.

Stem of clustered columns with collets attached to a rectangular central shaft.

At base, supporting brackets similar to those above affixed to a cruciform plinth. (sample description)

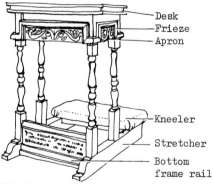

Desk
Frieze
Apron

Kneeler

Stretcher

Bottom frame rail

LITANY DESK, PRIE-DIEU or FALDSTOOL, not to be confused with a CREDENCE (side table)

Moulded stepped top rail.

Wrought-iron cylindrical supports (or standards) with spiral-twist centre sections between knots, and ivy decorated brackets splaying either side of upper two-thirds: hexagonal buttressed bases.

Bottom oak rail forms integral kneeler.

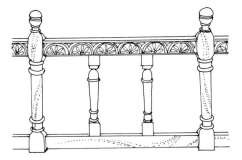

Moulded top rail with incised arcading on frieze.

Pillar-turned balusters between sturdier standards of the same shape which have cup and cover finials.

Grooved and domed bottom rail tenoned into bases of standards, the balusters resting on the rail.

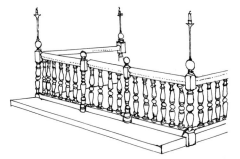

17th or 18th century LAUDIAN COMMUNION RAIL

(By the term 'Laudian' it is understood to enclose the altar.)

GALLERY (sometimes called a Tribune) with Balustrade consisting of groups of five turned balusters separated by fluted pilasters.

Festooned Frieze above lower Cornice.

A CHANCEL SCREEN divides the Chancel from the Nave (see PULPITUM, p.229).

A TOWER SCREEN separates the Tower and the Nave.

A PARCLOSE screens a Chapel or tomb from the Chancel or Nave.

Screens are usually divided into Bays with a pierced opening, sometimes with a gate. The outer bays are generally panelled at the base and open, except for the muntins, between the central rail and the top rail. The heads of the openings (called 'lights') mostly have carved tracery. The vertical outer frame members are known as 'stiles', the intermediate verticals being 'muntins'.

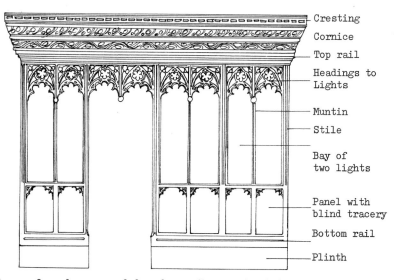

Cresting

Cornice

Top rail

Headings to Lights

Muntin

Stile

Bay of two lights

Panel with blind tracery

Bottom rail

Plinth

Square framed screen of four bays, the opening between the first and third bay on S side.

Heavy overhanging cornice crested with dentil moulding, below which are moulded fillets enclosing two bands of frieze, the upper one carved with pellets and gadrooning, the lower with an undulating vine: below are more bands of stepped moulding resting on the top rail.

Each bay contains two lights, between slender reeded muntins, with cinquefoil heads and pierced tracery beneath pointed arches with trefoil piercing in the spandrels of the upper arches.

The lower stage, either side of the passageway, has blind cinquefoil headed arches applied to the fielded panels.

All frame members have applied mouldings.

The screen stands on a deep and solid plinth with chamfered top edge.

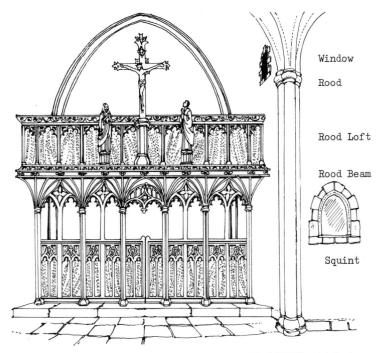

Window

Rood

Rood Loft

Rood Beam

Squint

A ROOD is sometimes embodied in the CHANCEL SCREEN, which is then referred to as the ROOD SCREEN.

Only the Cross and Crucifix is the Rood.

The Rood Loft is approached by a staircase and small door, usually on the North side. A small window high on the South side would light the Rood.

Traces of colour may be found and also interesting Corbels to support the Rood Beam.

The above ROOD SCREEN, of four bays, each with two-light cusped openings united with a central quatrefoil beneath an ogival head, is panelled at the base, the panels carved with blind trefoil headed arcading, the centre bay having a pair of doors.

Reeded posts carry the ribbed vaulting beneath the loft which is panelled, with a blind cusped arch in each of the twelve panels, and has a scrolled carved cornice.

The rood beam has thirteen carved floral bosses.

The Virgin Mary and St John, both with their hands clasped in prayer, their heads and shoulders protruding above the panelling, stand on reeded plinths.

The Corpus Christi with ... (see description of a CRUCIFIX) ... is integral with the floriated cross which is raised on an hexagonal pillar.

The ROOD SCREEN should not be confused with the PULPITUM which is built to the East of Rood Screens, but West of the choir, as a division between Nave and Choir; it usually spans the church and has a gallery.

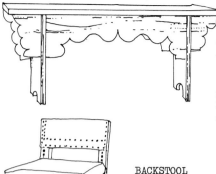

Oak FORM c.1520
of trestle construction

The apron (or underframing) which extends beyond the solid supports to the ends of the seat, is of ogee shape with rounded ends. The supports have grooved edges and arched openings below.
(sample description)

BACKSTOOL
first chair without arms,
term in use until late 18th century

Inventories distinguish between backstools, highstools, lowstools, footstools and chairs, which may be 'elbow' or 'back' chairs corresponding to 'arm' and 'side'.

FALDSTOOL (folding)
Early 17th century X-type

JOINED STOOL from c.1550

Four turned legs straddling outwards and united by a rail beneath the seat: linked just above floor level by stretchers.

When the legs are long they have been called, since the 19th century, COFFIN STOOLS.

Baroque STOOL with Spanish feet c.1690

One arched and scrolled stretcher,
two turned stretchers with squared
central section. (sample description)

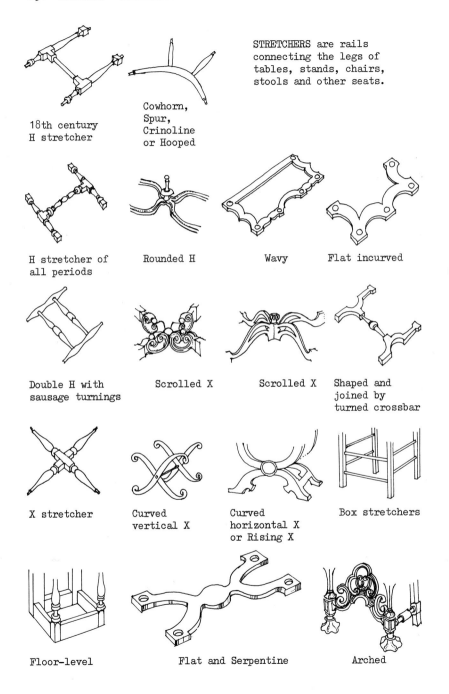

STRETCHERS are rails connecting the legs of tables, stands, chairs, stools and other seats.

18th century
H stretcher

Cowhorn,
Spur,
Crinoline
or Hooped

H stretcher of
all periods

Rounded H

Wavy

Flat incurved

Double H with
sausage turnings

Scrolled X

Scrolled X

Shaped and
joined by
turned crossbar

X stretcher

Curved
vertical X

Curved
horizontal X
or Rising X

Box stretchers

Floor-level

Flat and Serpentine

Arched

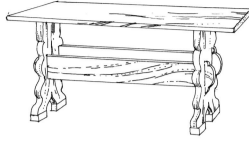

14th–16th century
TRESTLE TABLE

Oak with a pair of central
stretchers with protruding
ends secured by wooden
pegs.
Gothic-shaped pillar
trestles with ogee opening
at base.
Plank top.

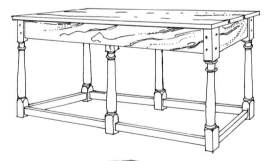

c.1600 Elizabethan oak
DRAW-LEAF TABLE

Moulded frieze with
deeply carved diagonal
gadroons.
Four bulbous legs, the
cups carved with
acanthus, the covers
nulled.
Square floor-level
stretchers.

c.1640 Jacobean
(oak or elm) TABLE

Six thin baluster legs
joined by square
stretchers. Top
formed by three
planks.

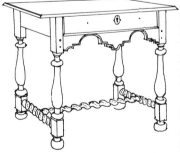

Oak SIDE TABLE with mixed features,
probably of 17th century country
origin

Inlaid banding of fruit wood let
into solid oak around top and drawer.

Wide apron rail of William and Mary
style with cock-beading around edge.

Neatly turned legs of baluster shape.

Joints pegged.

Barley-twist H stretchers.

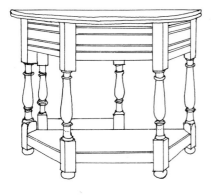

Oak CREDENCE c.1670

The frame of halved hexagonal
shape with circular top folded
in centre.

Gate at back with square
stretcher.
Six turned baluster legs.
Halved hexagonal bottom board.

N.B.   A Credence is a table
in a Sanctuary.

20th century CREDENCE of trestle form.

Moulded top-rail stretcher between plain
pillar trestles with canted corners, to which
is attached an ogee shaped apron carved with
cursive lilies.

Plain moulded domed bottom stretcher.

Stuart DRESSER c.1640

GATE-LEG TABLE c.1730

D-END TABLE c.1780

PEMBROKE TABLE c.1800

SOFA TABLE c.1820

ASH	Light brown with yellowish streaks.
BEECH	Pale, with a satiny grain, sometimes stained to resemble walnut. Used for country furniture and out of sight work.
ELM	Brown and tough, heavily grained - used for seats.
MAHOGANY	Dark, with a slight grain: not used before 1730.
MULBERRY	Yellowish brown, with dark streaks, heavy and tough, used in veneers.
OAK	Heavy and hard and darkens with age.
PINE	Yellow to red, soft and smooth. In use from 1660, especially for church seating. When pale, is often called 'yellow deal' - red called 'red deal'.
TEAK	Light or dark brown, heavy and durable. 20th century.
WALNUT	Antique British walnut has a honey-glow, but French and Italian is darker. Prone to woodworm. In use since 16th century.
YEW	Reddish to golden brown, very hard, used for country furniture.

Until c.1550 most furniture of oak, with walnut becoming popular in 16th century.

1649-60   (Cromwellian) Oak with leather upholstery.

1660-89   Oak, walnut, beech, cane, pine, veneers, marquetry.

1689-1702 As above with addition of gesso and lacquer.

1702-45   Mulberry and yew added and from 1730 mahogany.

1762-92   Satinwood introduced - fine inlays and painted furniture.

Very rough 'period' guide:

 500-1500 Anglo-Saxon and Mediaeval

1500-1660 Tudor and Early Stuart and Cromwellian 1649-60

1660-1714 Later Stuarts   Charles II   1660
                        William and Mary   1689
                              Queen Anne   1702

1714-1830 Georgian   Early Georgian and Baroque 1714-50
                       Chippendale and Rococo 1750-65
                       Gothick Revival mid 18th century
                       Adam, Hepplewhite and Neo-Classical c.1762-92
                       Sheraton 1790-1800
                       Regency 1800-30

1830-60   Early Victorian

1860-1914 Victorian and Edwardian

c.1900   Art Nouveau and other 20th century trends

Detailed charts on periods, types of furniture, constructional methods, materials and craftsmen are given in Gloag's 'A Short Dictionary of Furniture' - see Bibliography.

APPLIED   - work cut out from one piece of material and applied to
             the surface of another.
CARVING   - the material is cut out to leave shapes, which may be
             free-standing, in relief or pierced as in tracery.
INCISING   - a cut is made into the wood: a primitive term is
             scratch-carving.
INLAY, DAMASKEENING, INTARSIA, PARQUETRY - a design is cut out and
             inserted into prepared cavities on a surface.
MARQUETRY - a design is cut out and fitted into a sheet of veneer
             which is then applied, usually to an oak or pine
             carcase.
VENEER   - is a thin slither of fine wood glued to the surface of
             furniture for decorative effect.
MITRE   - diagonal joint formed by two mouldings.
BOARDED CONSTRUCTION - planks held in place by nails or pegged
             with oak pins at the angles and strengthened at each end
             with cross-pieces.
JOINED CONSTRUCTION is based on the use of the mortice and tenon
             joint.
MORTICE   - a cavity sunk in a member to receive a projection called
             a TENON on another, when the projection is fan-shaped
             the joint is termed DOVETAILED, when spiked it is
             DOWELLED, PEGGED or PINNED.
MOULDINGS - bands of wood of various shapes, each having a name of
             architectural origin (except for bead and quirk, bead
             and flush, and bead and butt). For CHAMFER see p.161.

BIBLIOGRAPHY

BRACKETT, O. (n.d.), 'English Furniture Illustrated', Hamlyn,
London.
FASTNEDGE, R. (1955), 'English Furniture Styles', Penguin,
Harmondsworth.
GLOAG, J. (1952), 'A Short Dictionary of Furniture', Allen & Unwin,
London. (Essential for NADFAS members and includes extensive date
charts and period styles.)
HAYWARD, C.H. (1971), 'English Period Furniture', Evans, London.
HUGHES, T. (1968), 'The Pocket Book of Furniture', Hamlyn, London.
JERVIS, S. (1976), 'Woodwork of Winchester Cathedral', The Friends
of Winchester Cathedral, Winchester.
JOY, E.T. (1967), 'The Country Life Book of Chairs', Hamlyn, London.
McDONALD, J.W. (1965), 'Antique Furniture', Collins, London.
McKAY, W.B. (1946), 'Joinery', Longman, London.
NEEDHAM, A. (1944), 'How to Study an Old Church', Batsford, London.
ROBERTSON, M. (1969), 'Going for a Song ...', BBC, London.
TEMPLE NEWSAM HOUSE, City of Leeds, Catalogues of Exhibitions of
Church Furniture.
VICTORIA & ALBERT MUSEUM (1971), London, Catalogue of 'Victorian
Church Art'.

600–1066	SAXON
1066–1199	NORMAN
1200–1539	GOTHIC

1170–1300	Early English	) overlapping
1272–1349	Decorated	) and still used
1350–1539	Perpendicular	) until c.1600

1485–1689	RENAISSANCE INFLUENCE

1485–1603	Tudor (1558–1603 Elizabethan)
1603–40	Early Stuart and Jacobean

1640–60	CROMWELLIAN – PURITAN (austere)
1660–1770	RESTORATION (reaction from above, foreign influences, Baroque, heavily ornamented)
1700–1800	QUEEN ANNE AND GEORGIAN (architectural influence predominating in everything, Rococo, light, gay, asymmetrical)
	c.1760 Birth of Gothick and Classical Revivals
1800–20	GOTHICK REVIVAL and CLASSICAL REVIVAL (Regency)
	1820–37 Degeneration of above
1837–1900	VICTORIAN (ornate copying of previous styles)
	c.1860 William Morris
	c.1890 Art Nouveau

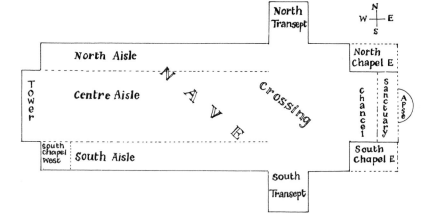

Mouldings are plain or enriched projecting or recessed bands, of ornamental value, either worked directly on a solid member (struck) or applied.

A member (such as a frieze or parts of a frame) with a cushion-like swelling is termed 'pulvinated'.

Band or Fillet

Astragal or Bead

Cavetto

Scotia

Ovolo

Torus

Ogee

Reverse Ogee

Moulding is 'bead and flush' when worked on all four sides of a panel, but 'bead and butt' when only two sides are beaded.

A quirk is a groove running parallel to a bead.

Flush bead

Bead and Quirk

Treacle (finger grip)

Bird's Beak

Toad Back

Stepped curve

Fluting

Reeding

INDEX

*indicates a sample description

Abacus, 2, 4, 5
Acanthus, 1, 50, 168
Achievement, 59, 76, 77, 85
Acolyte, 17
Acorn, 158, 160
Acroterion, 7
Aedicule, 8
Agnus Dei, 148
Alb, 181, 182
Alpha and Omega, 150
Alms bag, 171
    basin, 115*
    box, 202*
    dish, 115*
Altar, 153, 200*
Altar cross, 101*, 102-3*
Altar Tomb, 78
Amice, 181, 182
Amorini, 53
Angels, 143
Animals, 43
Antependium, 153
Anthemium, 50
Apparel, 181, 182
Applied, 86, 235
Apron, 8
Arabesque, see Moresque
Arcade, 3, 9, 159
Arch, 4, 9
Archaic words, 18
Archbishop, 182
Architectural plans and
    drawings, 128, 188
Architrave, 2, 5, 8
Armorial panel, 66
Armorials, 59, 96
Arms and armour, 19, 20, 21

Arms (coat of), 59, 60
Arms (royal), 68, 69
Arms of cross, 101
Asperges, 117*
Assay, 88
Astragal, 2, 237
Attic base, 1, 2
Aumbry, 162
Aureole, 101

Backplate, 114, 117
Backstool, 230
Badge, 59, 60, 69
Bag, 171
Baldachino, 221
Ball, 158, 159
Ballflower, 4, 50
Baluster, 97, 117, 154, 157,
    158, 225, 227
Balustrade, 7, 227
Bands, 54, 237
Banner, 170, 174
Baptismal shell, 116*
Baroque, 97
Barrel, 155, 157
Base, 2
Basketwork, 53, 73
Bay, 228, 229
Bayleaf, 50
Bead and Bead and reel, 50, 237
Beaker, 123
Beakhead, 4, 50
Beam, 6
Bedesman, 78
Bells, 129
Bell-shaped, 97, 154, 158

Bench, 201
Bequest board, 188
Bestiary, 127, 187
Bezel, 94, 95
Bi-axial, 58, 77
Bible box, 203*
Bible stories, 145
Bier light, 98*
Bifurcated, 50, 120, 121, 124-5, 155
Billet, 50
Biretta, 181
Blackamoor, 70
Black Letter, 72
Bladed, 160
Blazon, 59, 67
Blind, 3
Boat, 117*, 157
Bombé, 117, 157
Bookbinding examples, 15*, 16*
Bookbinding terms, 10-13
Bookmarkers, 171
Bookplate, 110
Boss, 6, 15, 127, 165
Bowl, 123, 157
Boxes, 202*, 203*
Brace, 6, 216
Bracket, 2, 8, 80-1, 163, 217, 221; see Consoles
Brass, 86
Brasses, 17, 22-3*, 75
Brattishing, 50
Bread oven, 162
Britannia metal, 86
British Hall Marks, 88
Broken, 5, 114, 159
Bronze, 86
Bucket, 117*, 127
Bucranium, 53
Bud, 158
Bulbous, 154, 218
Bun, 98, 158, 159
Burse, 171
Buttress, 5, 221

Cable, 50, 164
Cabochon, 128
Cadaver, 78
Cadency, 63
Cameo, 128
Candelabrum, 98*
Candle bracket, 114*
    extinguisher, 118*

stick, 97*, 98*, 99*
Canopy, 22, 80-1, 162, 164, 196
Canterbury, 71
Capital, 1, 2, 4
Capped, 159
Cardinal, 182
Carpet, 166-9
Cartouche, 58, 77, 86, 114
Carving, 235
Cassock, 181, 182
Cast, 86, 106
Cavetto, 237
Censer, 119*
Ceramics, 25, 26
Chair backs, 210, 211
Chairs, 204-9*
Chalice, 86, 88, 89-93*
Chamfer, 155, 161, 219
Chandelier, 111*
Chasing, 86
Chasuble, 181, 182, 183
Cherub, 53
Chest, 212-15*
Chevron, 50, 164
CHI RHO, 150
Chinoiserie, 53
Chip carving, 52
Chronogram, 74
Ciborium, 94*
Cinquefoil, 155, 156, 194
Circuminscribed, 95
Clasp, 15
Classical, 1, 4, 97
Clipped corner, 77, 88
Clocks, 29, 30*
Cloths, 170, 171
Clustered, 3, 4
Coat-of-arms, 22, 59, 60, 80-1
Coif, 34, 38, 182
Coins, 130
Collar beam, 6
Collection utensils, 127
Collet, 92-3, 99
Colonnade, 3
Colonnette, 3
Colours (heraldic), 61
    (regimental), 174
Column, 1, 2, 3
Communion cup, 86, 89*, 90*, 91*
    linens, 171
    rails, 227*
    veils, 171
Composite, 1
Compound, 3

Compressed, 160
Concave, 2, 103, 154, 155, 156
Concentric, 4
Cone, 99, 154, 156, 158, 168
Confessional pew, 224*
Consecration crosses, 187
Consoles, 221
Convex, 2, 154
Cope, 180*, 181, 184
Copperplate, 72
Corbel, 127, 163;
    inverted corbel, 102-3
Corinthian, 1
Cornice, 1, 2, 5, 8, 77
Corona, 1
Corona lucis, 112*
Coronet, 64
Corporal, 171
Costume, 31-41; see also
    Vestments
Counterflory, 53
Covered paten, 94
Covers, 158, 220*
Creatures, 43
Credence, 153, 163, 226, 233*
Cresset stone, 113
Crest, 59
Cresting, 124-5, 228
Crocket, 1, 4, 22-3, 116, 165
Crosses (basic), 100*, 101*,
    102*
Crosses (names of), 45-8
Crown, 7, 8, 64
Crozier, 118*, 181, 182
Crucifix, 49*
Cruciform, 116, 219
Cruet, 123
Crusader, 41
Cup, 122, 157
Cup and cover, 154, 160
Cupboard, 162
Cursive, 102-3*
Curtains, 173
Curvilinear, 195
Cushion, 1, 4, 173
Cusping, 53, 154, 196, 200
Cutcard, 124-5
Cylindrical, 97, 154, 157

Dado (die), 9, 192-3, 221,
    222
Dagger, 194
Dalmatic, 181, 182, 183

Date Letter, 88
Deacon, 17, 181
Decalogue, 188
Decorated period, 4
Decorative motifs, 50-3
Dentil, 1, 50
Desk, 109, 110, 225, 226
Dexter, 59, 66, 67
Diaper, 50
Diptych, 188
Dish paten, 96*
Dish-shaped, 157
Documents, 10
Dograil, 120
Dogtooth, 4, 50
Dome, 7, 158
Doorkeeper, 17
Doors, 216
Doric, 1, 2
Dormer, 7, 119
Dossal, 153, 170
Double cone, 50
Dragon vase, 26
Drawings, 128, 188
Dress, see Costume
Dresser, 233
Drum, 7, 154, 157, 225
Dumbell, 160

Early English, 4
Easter Sepulchre, 78, 162
Ecclesiastical clothing, see
    Vestments
Effigy, 78
Egg and tongue, dart, anchor,
    50, 51
Electroplate, 86
Elliptical, 117, 155
Embattled, 8, 51
Embossed, 86, 92, 115
Embroidery stitches, 176, 177,
    179
Enamel, 15, 87, 115
Encaustic tile, 27
EPBM, EPGS, EPNS, 87
Escutcheon, 7, 8, 63, 104-5
Evangelists' symbols, 22-3, 149
Ewer, 123
Exorcist, 17
Eye (oculus), 7

Facet, 92-3, 128

Faculty, 10
Fair linen cloth, 170, 171
Faldstool, 226, 230
Fall, 171
Feet, 159, 217
Feretory, 202*
Ferrule, 100, 118
Festoon, 51
Filigree, 128
Fillet, 2, 18, 34, 99, 237
Finger grip, 237
Finials, 94, 121, 123, 127, 158, 224
Fishtail, 121, 155
Flagon, 122*, 123, 124-5*
Flags, 174
Flamboyant, 195
Flange, 160
Flaring, 154
Fleur-de-lys, 15, 51, 149, 155
Floriation, 53
Flory, 53
Flowers, fruit and trees, 56, 57
Flower stand, 116*
Fluting, 52, 97, 237
Flying, 159, 221
Foils, 53
Foliage, 56, 57
Foliation, 53
Folio, 13
Font, 116*, 164*, 165*
Font covers, 220*
Foreign plate 'F', 88
Form, 230*
Foundries, 129
Fourleaf flower, 51
Frames, 58
Fresco, 186
Fret, 8, 51
Frieze, 1, 2, 5, 8, 232
Frontal, 153, 170
Fruit, 56, 57
Funeral armour, 24
    pall, 170
Furs, 61

Gable, 102-3, 109, 116
Gadroon, 51, 97, 232
Gallery, 116, 227
Garland or wreath, see Festoon, Swag
Gas lamp, gasolier, 114*
Gate, 120*

Gestures, 146
Girdle, 122, 181, 184
Glazing bars, 7
Gold Marks, 88
Gothic, 4, 160
Gothic lettering, 72, 92-3
Gothick Revival, 86
Gouge, 51
Graffiti, 187
Greek, 1
Greek lettering, 74
Green man, 44
Grotesque, 53
Guilloche, 51
Guttae, 2, 62, 217

Hagioscope, 162, 229
Halo, see Nimbus
Hammer beam, 6, 127
    post, 6
Hammered, 86, 91, 96, 117
Hand, 63, 146, 168
Handles, 104-5, 159
Hanging cross, 100
Hassock, 173
Hatched, 61, 87, 92-3, 124-5
Hatchment, 9, 66, 67*
Headdress, 35
Helmet, 20, 24, 65, 157
Heraldry, 59-71
Herse, 113
Hexagon, 155, 156, 160
Hinge, 107
Holy oil stocks, 115
Hood, 30, 181, 184
Hood-mould, 8
Hourglass, 127, 168
Husk, 51

Imbricated, 51, 98
Impale, 66, 67
Impost, 4, 5
Incense boat, 117*
Incised, 87, 235
Indent, 17, 76
Inlay, 235
Inscriptions, 18, 86, 92-3*, 190
Insignia, 59, 60
Interlace, 51
Intersection, 16
Ionic, 1

Iron, 106
Italic, 72

Jesse, 55
Jewellery, 86, 128
Jug, 123

Key, 108
Key escutcheon, 104-5
Key ornament, 8, 51
Kick-back, 26, 121
King post, 6
Kings, 142; Three Kings, 145
Kneelers, 173
Knight, Templar/St John, 41, 142
Knop: (ceramic) 26, (pewter) 87
Knop or Knot, 128, 160
Knot: (rug) 167, (lettering) 73

Label, 15, 16
Label stop, 8
Lace, 175
Ladle, 127
Lancet, 4, 194, 195
Language on brasses, 18
Lantern, 7, 113*
Lappets, 181
Latches and Locks, 108
Lattice, 51, 52
Laudian, 153, 170, 227
Lavabo jug and bowl, 123
    towel, 171
Lawyer (doctor), 41
Lectern, 109*, 226*
Lector, 17
Ledged, 216
Ledger, 75, 110
Legs, 218, 219
Lesene, 3
Lettering, 18, 72, 73, 74
Lids, see Covers
Lighting, 111*, 112*, 113*, 114*
Lights (window), 189, 194
Linens, 170-1
Lintel, 5
Lions (heraldic), 70
Litany Desk, 226
Lobed, 15, 51, 154, 159, 160
Lock, 108
Lombardic, 16, 72

Loop, 159
Lotus, 51
Louvre, 7
Lozenge, 51, 66, 77, 155, 206
Lucarne, 7
Lunette, 7, 51, 203, 206

Mace, 21, 127
Maniple, 171, 181, 182
Mantling, 60
Maps, 130
Marginal inscription, 22
Marks, ceramic, 25
    makers', 88
    masons', 187
    merchants', 17
    plate, 88
    window, 197, 198, 199
Marquetry, 235
Mask, 53, 164
Materials (textile), 178
Matrix, 18
Matted, 95, 117
Meander, 51
Measurements, 128
Medallions, 53, 84-5, 168, 169
Medals, 130
Menorah, 98
Mensa, 153, 163*
Metals, 61, 87
Metopes, 1, 2
Minutes, 10
Misericord, 223
Missal, 10
Missal stand, 110*
Mitre, 31, 181, 182, 207, 235
Models, 128
Mon-axial, 58, 82
Monks, 142
Monogram, 15, 16, 88, 95, 150
Monstrance, 119*
Moresque, 51, 95
Morse, 120*, 181, 184
Mortice, 235
Motto, 66, 67
Mouchette, 15, 124-5, 194
Moulding, 2, 4, 16, 161, 163, 227, 235, 237
Mount, 77, 123, 124, 125
Mozetta, 181, 182
Mullion, 194
Multifoil, 194
Multiknopped, 160

Muntin, 228
Mural, 29, 128
Mural crown, 60
Mushroom, 160
Music (sheet, etc.), 10
Musical instruments, 131-5
Mutules, 1, 2

Nailhead, 51
Nails, 106
Napery, 171
Natural leaf, 1
Neo-classical, 97
Niche, 8, 162
Nimbus, 152
Norman, 1, 4, 89, 107, 216
Nowy, 62, 77
Nulling, 51
Numbering of quartered shields,
    63
Numerals (Roman, Arabic), 74
Nuns, 142

Obelisk, 77
Octagon, 155
Oculus, 7
Oeil-de-boeuf, 7
Ogee, 4, 154, 194, 220, 237
Ogival compartment, 16, 154
Old Testament, 144
Omega, 150
Open, 5
Orb, 155, 158
Orders (classical), 1, 2
Orders of knighthood, 70
Organ, 134
Oriel, 7
Oriental rugs, 166-9
Ormolu, 87
Orphrey, 170, 181, 182, 184
Oval, 155
Oven, 162
Ovoid, 154, 157
Ovolo, 51, 237

Paintings, 188
Palimpsest, 17
Pall, 170
Palla, 171
Pallium (or pall), 181, 182
Palmette, 51

Panel, 15, 16, 216, 222
Parallelogram, 156
Paschal Lamb, 148
Passion (instruments), 151
Pastoral staff, 118*, 181, 182
Paten, 95*, 96*
Paten-Lid, 95*
Patera, 52
Pax, 115
Pear shaped, 154
Peardrop, 52
Pectoral cross, 100, 182
Pedestal, 7, 8, 84-5, 221
Pediment, 5, 7, 8, 77, 82
Pelican, 148
Pendant, 53, 225
Pennon, 174
Pentagon, 88, 155
Perforated, 117
Periods (woodwork), 234
Perizonium, 49
Perpendicular period, 4, 195
Persian rugs, see Oriental
Pew, 223*, 224*
Pewter, 87
Photographs, 128, 188
Pier, 3, 4, 9
Pierced, 52, 99, 222, 226
Pilaster, 3, 77
Pilaster strip, 3
Pilasterette/pilarette, 3
Pilgrim, 142
Pilgrims' crosses, 187
Pillar, 3, 9
Pin, 205, 235
Pinnacle, 4, 22, 116
Piscina, 162, 163
Plans, 128; church, 236
Plate, 86, 87, 195
Plate paten, 96*
Platinum, 88
Plinth, 2, 5, 164, 165, 221
Podium, 7
Polychrome, 128
Pomegranate, 121, 158
Poor Box, 202
Porcelain, 25
Portico, 7
Post, 6
Pottery, 25
Precatory scroll (or label), 18,
    22
Predella, 153
Pricket, 97, 113*

Prie-Dieu, 226
Priest, 182
Prints, 130
Prism, 156
Processional banner, 170*, 174
    cross, 100*
    torch, 98*, 112*
Prophets, 143
Province (Canterbury and York), 71
Pulpit, 225*, 226
Pulpit desk, 110*
Pulpitum, 229
Purificator, 171
Purlin, 6
Putti, 53, 83, 97
Pyramid, 155, 156
Pyx, 115

Quarries, 27, 194
Quatrefoil, 8, 53, 194
Queen post, 6
Quirk, 237

Radiating, 7
Rafter, 6
Rail, 201, 205, 216, 225, 228
Rails, 120*, 227*
Rat-tail, 121
Rebus, 22-3
Recess, 162
Rectilinear, 195
Reeding, 52, 97, 159, 237
Reel, 50
Registers, 10
Renaissance, 4
Repoussé, 86
Request Board, 188
Reredos, 153
Reserved, 87, 124-5
Respond, 9
Retable, 153
Reticulated, 16, 195
Return, 8, 9
Reveal, 161, 194
Rib, 164, 220
Ribbon (ribband), 15, 52, 83
Riddel, 170
Ridge, 6
Roll of Honour, 188
Roman, 1

Roman Lettering, 72
Rood, 229
Rood beam, 229
    screen, 229
Roof, 6
Rope (cable) moulding, 15, 164
Rose window, 7, 192
Rosette, 52
Roundel, 22-3, 53, 119, 164
Royal Arms, 68, 69*
Rugs, 166-9
Runner, 173
Running dog, 52, 168
Rushlight Holder, 113
Rustic, 54, 100

Sacred Monogram, see Monogram
Saints, 136-41
Salver, 96*
Sanctuary, 153
Sanctuary lamp, 112*, 153
Saracen and Savage, 70
Saucer dish, 96*
Saxon, 4
Scallop, 1, 4, 52
Sceptre, 152
Sconce, 114*
Scoop, 51
Scotia, 2, 237
Scratchwork, 52
Screen, 228*, 229*
Screws, 106
Script, 72
Scroll, 49, 52, 106, 159, 187, 204
Sculptors, 79
Seal, 16
Secco, 186
Sedilia, 163
Sees, 71
Segmental, 4, 5
Sentences, 186
Sexton, 17
Shaft, 1, 2, 3, 4, 23, 164
Shamrock, 16, 69
Shapes (basic), 154-60
Sheffield plate, 87
Shell, 52, 116, 142, 155
Shield, 15, 62, 63, 80-1, 121, 147, 211
Shoulder, 77, 154, 160
Shrouded figure, 17
Sigmoid, 77, 154

Signs and symbols, 146-52
Silver Marks, 88
Silver Plate, 87
Silverplated, 87
Sinister, 59
Skeleton, 17
Sketches, 188
Skirt, 159
Skirting, 221
Socle, 157
Soffit, 8
Spandrel, 9, 30, 95
Sparrowbeak, 26
Spherical, 155, 160
Spiral, 160
Splat, 208
Splayed, 154, 161, 219
Spool, 95
Spoon, 117
Springing, 8
Sprinkler, 117*
Spur, 5
Squint, 162, 229
Staff, 118*, 152, 181
Stained glass, 196
Stall, 223*
Stamps (marks), 129
Stamps, 130
Stand, 203
Standard, 152, 174
Staple, 108
Stars, 150, 168
Stations of the Cross, 145, 188
Steeple, 120, 158
Stepped, 92-3, 159, 237
Sterling mark, 88
Stiff Leaf, 1, 4, 164
Stile, 216, 228
Stitches, 176, 177, 179
Stole, 171, 181, 182
Stool, 230*
Stoup, 117*, 162
Strapsconce, 113
Strapwork, 51, 52, 58, 95
Stretchers, 231
Stud, 159
Styles, 236
Stylobate, 7
Sun motif, 95
Superfrontal, 153, 170
Supports, 1, 3
Surplice, 181
Swag, 52
Swan-necked, 5, 122

Swelling, 160
Sword-rest, 127

Tabernacle, 116*, 153, 161
Tables, 232*, 233*
Table-tomb, 78, 80-1*
Tablet, 2, 75, 77, 82
Tankard, 122*
Tapering, 97, 154
Tazza, 96
Techniques, see entry at end of
    index
Tenon, 235
Terminal, 121, 123
Terminology, see entry at end of
    index
Terrier, 10
Texts, 142, 190
Textured, 100
Thistle, 69, 154
Thumbpiece, 87, 121, 124-5
Tiara, 181
Tie beam, 6
Tiles, 27, 28*
Tinctures, 61
Toad Back, 237
Tongs, 127
Torch, 112*
Torchère, 116*
Tortoise, 168
Torus, 2, 237
Touch (pewter), 87
Tracery, 52, 124-5, 194, 195
Transitional, 1
Transom, 194
Trapezium, 156
Treacle, 237
Tree of Jesse, 55
Tree of Life, 63, 169, 187
Trefoil, 53, 155, 156, 194
Trellis, 52
Triangle (triangular), 5, 155,
    156
Tribune, 227
Tricking, 59, 67*
Triglyph, 1, 2
Trinity, 147, 152
Tripod, 98, 159
Triptych, 153, 188
Trophy, 54
Trumeau, 8
Trumpet-shape, 159
Truncated, 154

Truncheon, 127
Truss, 6, 220
Tuck-in base, 159
Tudor flower or ornament, 4, 51, 52
Tudor rose, 4, 52, 69
Tunicle, 181, 182
Tuscan, 1, 2
Tympanum, 7, 8
Types and Antitypes, 143

Underglaze, 25
Undulate band, 54
Union Jack, 174
Urn, 157, 158

Vase, 26*, 117, 157, 208
Veils, 171, 172
Vellum, 12
Veneer, 235
Vernicle, 95
Vertebrate band, 54
Vessels, 123
Vestments, 181-4
Vexillum, 174
Viaticum, 123
Vine, 52, 187
Vitruvian scroll, 52
Volute, 1, 4, 121, 155, 204
Vowess, 34, 81

Wafer box, 115
Wagon roof, 6
Wainscot, 222
Waisted, 158
Wall Memorial, 82*, 83*, 84-5*
Wall Painting, 186, 187
Wall plate, 6, 114
  post, 6
Wand, 118*

Wares, 25
Waterleaf, 1, 52, 106, 114, 120
Watermark, 130
Weepers, 78
Wheelcross, 100
Wheel window, 7
Window Marks, 197, 198, 199
  plan, 189
  sample descriptions, 191*, 192-3*
  tracery, 195
Wings, 77, 82, 143
Woods, 234
Words from the Cross, 145
Wrought iron, 106, 111
Wrythen, 89, 160

York, 71

TECHNIQUES and TERMINOLOGY
at a glance

architectural, 1-9
books, 10-11
brasses, 19-21
clocks, 29-30
costume, 31-41
decorative, 50-4
frames, 58
heraldic, 59-71
jewellery, 128
lettering, 72-4
memorials, 76-8
metal, 86-7
rugs, 168-9
stitches, 176-9
stonework, 161
vestments, 181-4
windows and tracery, 194-6
wood, 235